FRIEND

# WHAT WOULD I DO WITHOUT THEM?

Finding Real And Valuable Friendships In An Unfriendly World

**Emma S. Etuk, Ph.D.**

Emida International Publishers
Washington, D.C. - Uyo, Nigeria

## Publisher's Cataloging-in-Publication
### (Provided by Quality Books, Inc.)


Etuk, Emma S., 1948-
    Friends : what would I do without them? :
finding real and valuable friendships in an
unfriendly world / Emma Samuel Etuk. -- 1st ed.
    p. cm.
    Includes bibliographical references and index.
    ISBN: 1-881293-02-5

    1. Friendship. 2. Friendship--Religious
aspects--Christianity. I. Title.

BJ1533.F8E88 1999        177'.62
                QBI99-768

For additional copies, contact:

Emida International Publishers
P. O. Box 50317,
Washington, D.C. 20091.

ISBN: 1-881293-02-5

Cover design by George Foster
Book design and typesetting by Matthew Sadiku
This book is composed in Garamond

Printed in the USA by

MORRIS PUBLISHING

3212 East Highway 30 • Kearney, NE 68847 • 1-800-650-7888

Dedicated to:

*ALL MY PRECIOUS FRIENDS WORLDWIDE*

*without whom my life would have been a misery*

*and a terrible failure.*

# PREFACE

Throughout my half a century years of life, I have come to know so many people: family members, professional colleagues, school and college-mates, members of the churches that I have attended, acquaintances and persons I simply have run into in the course of life's bustling activities.

As much as I can remember, I have written letters to hundreds of people. In one Christmas season, I mailed out over one hundred letters. In all likelihood, I also have received hundreds of letters. I have tried to keep the most of these. I possess a long mailing list on various people whom I have come into contact with.

But all these people are not truly my friends. This is a basic problem of life. We meet and associate with very many people but we cannot make all of them our friends. In the cosmopolitan and highly urbanized world of the 1990's, you and I know what it feels like to be among a sea of faces who are not friends.

I believe that you, too, have had a similar experience. You know exactly what I mean. You live in a large apartment complex. Or, you are a college student residing in a dormitory. Or, still, you own a personal home. You may be part of the working population. You may even be heading right now to a church conference attended by thousands of people. But, deep within you, you are sad and lonely. Because you know that you have no real and valuable friends. "Where have all the good people gone to?" you may be asking yourself. My book will help you to discover them if you believe that friendship is vitally important. The people who can be your friends are all around you.

My interest in writing this book began a long time ago, about 1990, after I had published my second book, *A Walk Through the Wilderness* in which I narrated some of my earliest experiences in the United States as a foreign student. I had noted in that book that it was hard for me to make real and valuable friendships because I had observed that Americans are individualists. They seem to dearly cherish their aloneness.

My research at the time revealed that many people in the United States were loners. I wanted to examine this subject in some detail, for my own sake, and for the sake of the millions traveling through the American wilderness of loneliness. Now, nearly after nine years, I have done my investigation.

Friendship involves risk-taking, being vulnerable. I have examined this subject within the context of love and sex. I truly believe that part of the problem about contemporary modes of friendship is that relationships in America are highly sexualized. Love has been trivialized and many people fail to find good friends because there is little room for platonic love today.

The pressure is great. The Hollywood culture has reinforced this trivialization of love and Hollywood is partly responsible for the pressures that we all have to face. How often is it that you find two people on television promoting platonic love? Yet, even in secular literature, we can find examples of true friendships. There are the cases of Romeo and Juliet, Pythias and Damon, in the ancient classics.

In this book, I have pointed to the examples of David and Jonathan, Ruth and Naomi, in the Bible. You, yourself, may even recall some cases of true friendship that you may have noticed during your lifetime. But, you may not have taken the time to consider them. It is important that we re-consider such friendships and celebrate them. Because friendships are the necessary spices which add enrichment to our lives.

The scheme of this book begins with the assertion that everyone needs a friend (Chapter One). In Chapter Two, I discuss the meaning of a real friendship. I draw examples and insights from both secular and sacred literature. "Friendship in Lonely America" is analyzed in the third chapter. In Chapters Four and Five, I deal specifically with friendships in terms of gender: female-female and male-to-male friendships. The next four chapters analyze friendships in the home, the workplace, the church and the schools and colleges.

In Chapter Ten, I examine the controversial issue of race and racism and provide an analysis on how we can have friendships across racial lines. The last Chapter Eleven provides twelve benefits that one can have from a true friendship. In my conclusion, I insist that divine friendship ought to be our goal. I confess that Jesus Christ is and will continue to be my best friend. He won me over by His love for me.

People who are blessed with many friends are truly rich. My perspective is an Ibibio perspective, which I share with you as an African. I hope that after you have completely read this book, it will prompt you to think seriously about having some good friends and about becoming a truly good friend to someone else. Thus, you and I will be contributing toward making this world a better place than we found it.

ESE
March 16, 1999

# ACKNOWLEDGMENT

First and foremost, thank you, GOD, for the ability, perseverance, persistence, vision and wisdom to write this book. Often we forget that all our endeavors and successes are a result of divine grace and benevolence. Without God's enablement, the writing of this book would not have been completed.

When this book was started in 1996 in Daytona Beach, Florida, there were hurts and pain in my life. There was disappointment and hopelessness and I feared for the future. It is God alone who helped me to turn my scars into stars. He turned things around for me. So, GOD, thank you very much.

Writing a book involves a lot of monetary expense. There have been persons who stood with me throughout this arduous exercise, persons who provided the finanacial assistance necessary for the continuance and completion of this book. I wish to acknowledge them here: the dentist, Dr. Mfon E. Umoren, Dr. Ekwere Ifon, Barbara and John Ricketts, Ben Dadson, Zelma Wilson, Dr. Matthew Sadiku, Dr. Nseobong Aquaowo, Edwin and Bimpe Quartey, and the Gambrahs.

Others include Dr. Alusine Jalloh, Dr. Efre F. Ekpo, Kwasi Frempong, Carolyn Saxon, Rev. A. B. K. Appiah, Steve Onu, Tom Mbeke-Ekanem, and Francisco Castillo. Some names must remain anonymous. But I sincerely thank these benefactors and encourage them to continue their support as we produce and provide more literature materials needed in our communities.

No author can succeed today in the book industry without some mechanism to market his or her books. I have been very fortunate to have great helpers like Dr. Bolu Olowomeye, Paul Glenn of the Adventist Bookstore in Takoma Park, Maryland, Joseph Richardson of the African Christian Fellowship in Baltimore, Rev. Stephen Ogunjimi, Ojimadu Okoronkwo, Rev. Dr. C. Anthony Muse and Don Courtes of the Resurrection Prayer Bible College, pastor Eyo Umoh of Dallas, pastor Tony Perkins, Joycelyn Gordon and Rev. Jacob Rodawla.

Others worthy of mention are Dr. Chim and Edna Ogbonna of the Oversea Brethren Fellowship, Veronica Ekweonu, Dr. George Utuk, Rev. J. Cruz, Rev. Dr. T.A. O. Agbeja of the Christ Apostolic Church, Bob and Angelika Selle, Rev. Quentin Poulson, Rhoi Wangila of the Ark Foundation of Africa, Greg Banks, and my pastor Rev. Stephen Gyermeh. I should not forget Rev. K. O. Gyimah for his enthusiasm about my work and encouragement. I am really grateful for your support.

Specific mention must be made of Dr. Sulayman Nyang of Howard University and Dr. Percy Thomas, Provost at the Montgomery Community College in Rockville, Maryland. These two friends provided and continue to provide me with access to television. In this regard, I should mention the late Dr. James Moone, former president of the Maryland Chapter of the Southern Christian Leadership Conference (SCLC), for his radio interview and fervent interest in my books. The African and African-American communities lost a great leader when Moone passed into eternal bliss in early 1999. I miss him very much.

I shared this writing wholly or in part with some friends, for their advice and insights. These include Dr. Winona Somervill and Dr. Gery Eli of Dillard University in New Orleans, Dr. Henry Efesoa-Mokossa of the Southern University of New Orleans, the Hon. Bob McDermott of the state of Hawaii, Dr. Robert B. Sloan, Jr., president of Baylor University in Waco, Texas, Dr. Alvin Anderson, Dr. Sulayman Nyang, the Purnells, Dr. K. Osia, Dr. JoAnn Perkins, Elaine Saunders, Dr. Emmanuel and Grace Akpan, and Dr. Edna N. Sims of the University of the District of Columbia.

Other people whom I must mention in this respect are Ms. Julia Dinkins, Janice Davis and Tamara Shockley (both attorneys), Dr. George Ayittey (himself a prolific writer), Ime and Mary Ekanem, Dr. Geoffrey Tetteyfio, Anna F. Towns, Clark and Edith Jones, Dr. Leonard Lempel (a wonderful encourager), Dr. Nancy Long, Dr. J. A. Ampiaw, Dr. Dorothy Autrey, Tony Oyatedor, Dr. Stephen Olford (my spiritual mentor), Dr. Bob and Connie Smeltzer (friends for 19 years), Ms. Ikwo Ekpo, Dr. Johnetta Davis, and Esme Bhan (the kindest woman I have known in the academic circles).

Still more names: Stephanie Stamm, Sandra C. Hayes, Marla H. Lundberg, Pauline M. Kurin, Dr. C. F. Ndege, Laura Spedding, Cathy D. Washington, Lisa Fishman (thank you for your comments), Dr. Sam Oli, Ms. Cherie Houston, Dr. John Ukawuilulu, Jim Wallis, Dr. Daniel Stowell, Rev. Ron Kimble, Snr., Dr. Caroline

Simon, Helen Okpokowuruk, Lorine Butler, Latasha Lawrence ("princess"), Tracey Cohen (thanks for the typing), former Sen. Carol Moseley-Braun, and Bill Clinton, president of the United States of America. In one way or another, this is the book which you all have helped me to write. I have benefited from your collective wisdom.

During the process of completing this book, the Women's Fellowship of the Church of the Living God at 1417 Chillum Road in Hyattsville, Maryland, was the first in 1996 to offer me an opportunity to test out my ideas before a live audience. Therefore, I must thank their president, Angela Appiah, for that generosity. The evaluation which I made of the reception of the material in Chapter Four, which I shared then, strengthened my conviction that this kind of book would reach a wider audience. Later, in 1998, I also addressed members of the National Pentecostal Holiness Church on this subject of friendship. The congregation is led by Rev. Tony Perkins. Thank you, brother Perkins.

Dr. Christian C. Nwachukwu of the Africa Solidarity Council, Inc., Dr. Oswald P. Bronson, Snr., president of Bethune-Cookman College in Daytona Beach, Florida, and Dr. Stanley J. Drake, founder and president of the International Society of Friendships and Good Will (ISFGW) graciously provided the back-cover blurbs and recommendations. I am really grateful.

Kathie Scriven did an excellent editorial work polishing the manuscript. Her contribution greatly improved my writing. I highly recommend her to anyone who desires her services. And, George Foster, my artist and designer, did a wonderful and professional work on the covers. His expertise and talent speak for themselves. My college-mate, Paul Mills of the Martin

Luther King, Jr. Library in Washington, D.C. assisted me in the discovery of materials for the analysis of friendships in schools and colleges. Thank you.

Finally, I want to thank Mimi and Ini, my children and future hope. They have been involved in all the agonies and thrills of producing this book. Ini, my four-years-old son, has already claimed this book his own. In some sense, it is his book. Last but not the least, I thank Ayda, my spouse, for the wonderful help in "fixing" the manuscript when I got completely frustrated with my ignorance regarding the use of the computer. I thank you Ayda for your understanding and constant support. To God be all the glory, honor, and praise.

# CONTENTS

Dedication ii

Preface iii

Acknowledgements vii

1. Everyone Needs A Real Friend 1

    The Wonderful Friend from Missouri
    My Personal Experiences
    Glimpses from "Coming to America."
    Mathabane comes to America
    Friendless Jailbirds
    Friendless Runaways and Prostitutes
    Friendless Campuses
    Men Without Friends
    A Nation of Strangers

2. The Meaning of a Real Friend 17

    Perspectives on Friendship
    Cicero on Friendship
    Solomon on Friendship
    Montaigne on Friendship
    Lewis on Friendship

Montaigne on Friendship
Lewis on Friendship

## 3. Friendship in Lonely America     39

Literature on Loneliness
A Typical Scenario
Meaning of Loneliness
Three Giants Who Faced Loneliness
The Cost of Loneliness
Friendship: Antidote for Loneliness

## 4. Woman-to -Woman Friendships     55

Ruth's Profile
Naomi's Profile
Their Bond of Friendship

## 5. Man-to-Man Friendships     69

Jonathan's Profile
David's Profile
Their Bond of Friendship

## 6. Friendships in the Home     93

Husband and Wife Friendship
Child-Parent Friendship
Friendship Among Children

Extended Family Friendship

7. **Friendships at the Workplace**  111

Conventional Workplace Environment
Return to Work Friendships
Examples of Work Friends
Corporations Enhancing Friendship

8. **Friendships at Church**  129

Noisy Assembly, Friendless People
Vibrant Organism, Weak Organization
Personal Experiences
Spiritual Friendships
Some Practicals

9. **Friendships at Schools and Colleges**  155

Saturated Brains, Empty Hearts
A Friendlier, Kindlier Education
Act Now
Some Practical Suggestions

10. **Friendships Across Racial Lines**  177

The Meaning of Race
What is Racism
Building Friendship Across Racial Lines

## 11. The Benefits of Friendship   201

A great support system
Antidote for loneliness
Personal uplift
Ally
Assistance
Proper childhood development
Catalyst for love
Life's enrichment
Self-discovery
Liberation
Longevity
Networking

## 12. Conclusion   223

Notes   229
About the Author   263
Index   265

# CHAPTER ONE

## EVERYONE NEEDS
## A REAL FRIEND

*It is great to have friends when one is young, but indeed it is still more so when you are getting old.*

— Edvard Grieg

### The Wonderful Friend From Missouri

Remember the wonderful man from the state of Missouri who rose from obscurity on a farm to become one of the world's most celebrated men? His name was Dale Carnegie, author of many books, celebrated for his many training institutes, a great public speaker, and a financial success.

At the beginning of his adult life, Carnegie was not a great industrialist. He was no great philosopher. He was not even a graduate from one of the Ivy League colleges or universities. He became a great success, however, despite his not having many credentials. How did he do it? What was his secret?

Dale Carnegie achieved international fame by discovering the way to help millions of people fill a vital, universal, human need -- friendship. In 1906, Carnegie was a junior at State Teachers College in Warrensburg, Missouri. His own family was poor. The prospect for great success was slim. But young Carnegie knew within himself the great importance of using an idea to assist people build their self-esteem and confidence.

As Carnegie began to believe in himself, he soon discovered that he could believe in people, that is, *he could win friends and influence people.* He realized that he could sell himself as a nice guy, a really nice guy, a good friend. Six years later, Dale Carnegie was teaching and sharing his ideas of human relationships with the Y.M.C.A. Within a few months, his teaching classes proved to be so popular that other Y.M.C.A.s wanted his course in their adult education programs.

In 1933, Leon Shimkin, president of Simon and Schuster, Inc., today a major publishing company, enrolled in one of Carnegie's classes in Larchmont, New York. Shimkin was so impressed with it that he suggested to Carnegie to put all his ideas into a book. The result was the publication of the phenomenal bestseller, *How To Win Friends And Influence People*[1] on November 12, 1936. This book has helped millions of people find happiness and success.

Carnegie's book sold over one million copies within the first year of its publication. By 1964, a total of over 8.4 million copies had been sold! In 1996, I walked into a Books-A-Million bookstore in Daytona Beach, Florida, to purchase this book but it was unavailable -- sold out. Today, any wise CEO would keep a copy of *How To Win Friends* at his desk or on his bookshelf. Carnegie had found out that men and women, all over the world, need friends. The phenomenal success of his book underscores the fact that people truly desire to have friends in their lives and recognize this need.

It has been over ninety years since Dale Carnegie first recognized the importance of human relationships and the necessity to promote friendships. Our need for friends and friendships has not disappeared nor diminished since then. Unfortunately, however, a lot of people are still friendless. Many people in retirement homes and institutions have no friends. Scores of thousands, and perhaps, even millions of refugees in our world have no friends. In many prisons, the convicts have no friends. Even many college students and churchgoing people I have met have no real or very few friends.

How often do we hear a former gang member say that he or she loved the gang because gangs are like a family, providing a sense of belonging and protection. Their relationships are based upon loyalty and friendship. The gangs provide the gangster with the kind of friends that encourage and care. It is no wonder that one group of gangsters would be willing to war against any other opposing group and even be willing to kill in order to protect their own!

## My Personal Experiences

In one of my previous books, *A Walk Through The Wilderness* (1990), I narrated the experiences which I had when I first arrived in the United States in August of 1980 from Nigeria. Oh, what false images of America I had had previous to coming here -- that it was a land flowing with milk and honey; a land where everyone drove a big car and where money, literally, grew on trees. I had been told that America was "God's Country" and that Americans were very friendly and hospitable.

I was in for a culture shock. My plane landed at John F. Kennedy Airport in New York, at the Pan Am exit. It was only a few minutes after leaving the Customs that a taxicab driver cheated me and took several of my traveler's checks for a ride which should have cost me only five dollars from the J.F.K. airport to LaGuardia, another nearby airport.

In the course of the last eighteen years, I have traveled to several states and taken up residences in many dormitories and apartments. I have resided in Canton and Ashland, Ohio; in Waco, Texas; in Washington, D.C., in Riverdale, Maryland; in New Orleans, Louisiana; and in Daytona Beach, Florida. I have resided in Maryland with my wife and children in the same apartment complex for over a decade.

I know from personal experience how friendless and lonely life can be in this country. I know what it is like to reside in a large apartment complex, with hundreds of tenants living with their own families, and still be without any true and real friends. And, I'm a Christian who regularly attended church during that period of time. I am not the only one who has had this kind of experience.

My quest for higher education and my career as a college professor have also led me to travel a lot across the United States by the Greyhound buses and Amtrak trains. I have listened to hundreds of persons in conversations. I have observed the American social scene and lifestyle as I teach and speak in many churches. I have taught history at four historically black colleges and universities.

Also, I attended three predominantly white institutions of higher education in Canton and Ashland, Ohio, and in Waco, Texas. I can safely state that, generally speaking, many Americans have few or no permanent friends. Also, *platonic* relationships appear to be obsolete. Relationships in America are highly sexualized. America is a wilderness of loneliness.

Abigail Van Buren ("Dear Abby"), in the Daytona Beach, Florida, *News Journal* of March 15, 1996, published a letter from one Jack Pletman of Huntington Station, New York. The letter was about "Neighbors [who] Remain Strangers Through 25 Years of Living." Pletman revealed that he had a decent, respectable family. In the twenty-five years of residing in Huntington, Pletman said, events such as births, graduations, weddings, and deaths came and went with no acknowledgment from his next-door neighbor. Upon reflection Jack Pletman said: "We are all poorer for having ignored one another, but we survived."

Van Buren commented: "Neighbors need each other today for security as well as for the sake of old-fashioned friendship." She added: "This is a plea for people to reach out and offer their friendship to the newcomers in the neighborhood. And if the welcome is slow in coming, the newcomers should initiate the dialogue. Nothing separates like silence."

Author Vance Packard in his book, *A Nation of Strangers*, writes about one woman who described how she felt when she first moved into a neighborhood in Darien, Connecticut: "No one on the lane of some twenty-two families phoned or called in person to welcome us to the community. We have been here a year and have only a nodding acquaintance with the neighbors

-- and not all of them."[2]

Another woman said: "I have found it most difficult to make friends since moving to Darien. I am not speaking of bosom friends -- just casual acquaintances."[3] A house wife residing in Azusa, California, told Packard: "I've been here a year and two adults have spoken to me from this neighborhood."[4] Bear in mind that this woman was not an old, shut-in retiree. She was an active wife of a computer programmer.

The Darien woman who lived in a community of twenty-two families disclosed that her long distance telephone bills ran very high during her first two months as she struggled to reconnect with her former friends back home in Texas. A similar thing happened to me when I temporarily relocated to New Orleans in 1992 and to Daytona Beach in 1995, leaving my family in Riverdale, Maryland.

In Daytona Beach, Florida, I had an unforgettable experience. Before taking up residence at a particular Sandy Park apartment complex, I had gone over to the complex to "connect" with some residents there. I met a black couple sitting at a verandah one evening. When I tried to introduce myself as a prospective new tenant, they gave me such hostile looks that plainly told me that I was not welcome. I was shocked at their lack of hospitality.

I was embarrassed because I considered them "my people" -- the people of my own race from whom I expected, at least, a casual friendship. The day I moved in, a white woman, probably in her early seventies, promptly knocked at my door. She introduced herself as being my next door neighbor and that I was very welcome. I later found out that she was a sweet lady by the name of Jocelyn Hutchinson. We remained friends until I left Daytona Beach.

## Glimpses from "Coming to America"

Did you ever see Eddie Murphy's movie, "Coming to America?" When the two leading characters in this movie arrived for the first time in the United States, they were not greeted by warm, open hands of hospitality. The two visitors first took up residence in a neighborhood in Queens, New York. It was not long before many of their pieces of luggage were stolen.

The landlord of their apartment took pride in exploiting the new arrivals. The women they met tried to seduce and dupe them. Soon, the two immigrants ran out of money. They had played the prodigal, sowing their "royal oats," in a country where many neighbors hardly know each other nor trust each other.

I have found that many Americans do not even know the names of their next door neighbors. In this kind of environment, how can one find a real friend? You really have to work hard at it if you care to. Eddie Murphy's film is a fictional depiction of the friendless environment in which we live. Let me offer you an example of the experiences of another immigrant.

## Mathabane comes to America

Many immigrants who arrive in America are often bewildered by a "friendless America." Unfortunately, however, they soon adopt this friendless American lifestyle. It is absolutely incredible how many African immigrants I meet who complain that America is a very lonely place. Yet, even though these same immigrants want friends, they do not keep permanent friends. They quickly adapt to the American lifestyle of loosely-held relationships.

Mark Mathabane, author of four books and, particularly, of the bestseller *Kaffir Boy: The True Story of A Black Youth's Coming of Age in Apartheid South Africa* now resides in Kernesville, North Carolina, with his wife and two children. On September 16, 1978, at the age of eighteen, Mark left apartheid South Africa on a tennis scholarship and arrived the following day in the United States to study at Limestone College in Gaffney, South Carolina. When his jumbo jet landed at Atlanta's International Airport, Mark found himself "alone in a foreign land, with no family or friends, no wise mother to give me sound advice."[5]

Like me and many other foreign students, Mark soon made some initial "friends," actually acquaintances, in a college that had no African or African-American professors and where the farceness of American integration added to the multiplicity of his confusion about American freedom and democracy. Mark wrote: "I was anxious to make friends, to be liked. But I was unwilling to pay any price for friendship, for popularity."[6] In his case, "the price" would have meant conformity with the marijuana - smoking and liquor drinking habits of his college roommate.

To make matters worse, Mark had to resist the temptation to settle for the wild-partying lifestyle of his tennis playmates. His culture shock worsened with each passing day. When Mark dated girls without having sexual intercourse, his college-mates gossiped around that he was homosexual, that something must be wrong with him, or that he was effeminate.

Even some black-American students accused Mark of seeking to be white because he was studious. I analyzed

Mark's experiences during the first four months of his stay in the United States and found that Mark had three or four persons who really cared about him. David Mark Bonar, a black-American student was one. Reverend J.W. Saunders of the local Bethel Baptist Church was another. Mark's sponsors, Stan (and his wife Margie) Smith were the other pair. The rest of the Limestone College community were simply acquaintances or associates.

I really doubt whether Ron Killion, Mark's tennis coach, was anything other than a paternalist, given his attitude toward Mark Mathabane. Consequently, Mark's depression and homesickness increased. He began to develop self doubt. His relationship with Ron Killion and the tennis team deteriorated. He became withdrawn, antisocial and uncommunicative. In the cafeteria, Mark often sat alone and brooded. You can say he was daydreaming.

Finally, Dr. Ron Killion and the tennis team ousted Mark from their company. By the end of the first semester, Mark lost his scholarship even though he maintained a G.P.A. of 3.11. He was forced to quit Limestone College. His case is an example of the effect of friendlessness upon any new immigrant to America.

## Friendless Jailbirds

Why do you think many people hate to go to prison? Certainly there are many reasons. At least one reason is because they instinctively understand that prisons are not friendly environments. Merlin Carothers of Ellwood City, Pennsylvania, wrote the bestseller, *Prison To Praise*, in 1970 which has been reprinted seventy-four times since then, with thirteen million copies in print. In this

book, Merlin describes how he was arrested for deserting
the army and for armed robbery. He spent six months in
jail at Fort Benning, Georgia and at Fort Dix in New
Jersey.

He received a five-year temporarily suspended jail
term sentence from a federal judge in Pittsburgh. He was
only nineteen and in search of life's excitements when he
was first arrested and/or jailed. Merlin wrote: "I had to
suffer the humiliation of the jail cell... the lonely cell and
the hard bunk with nothing to do but stare at the wall."[7]
This was before he became a U.S. paratrooper in World
War II, serving two years in Europe.

Merlin returned from Europe to become a Christian
minister. He also received a presidential pardon from
Harry Truman. For Merlin, time in jail was friendless and
fearful. Prison culture has been described by Charles W.
Colson who, before his incarceration, was president
Richard Nixon's special counsel.

On June 22, 1974, *The Washington Post* told the entire
world: "Colson Gets 1-to-3 Year Term." Judge Gessell
had ordered the previous day that "the court will impose
a sentence of one to three years and a fine of five
thousand dollars."[8] This was the punishment for Chuck
Colson's role in the Watergate affair.

Colson had become a Christian during this national
crisis which rocked the American presidency like nothing
else had ever before. But now Colson was about to face a
friendless, cold, lonely "slammer" at Fort Holabird, in
Baltimore, Maryland and at the Maxwell Airforce Base in
Montgomery, Alabama. Of his Baltimore jail experience,
Colson wrote: "My need for special inner strength was
heightened by my loneliness, my daily uneasy encounters
with members of organized crime, and feelings of despair
about the future. Always the threat of physical assault by

another inmate hung over me."

One night Colson was scared to death as he suspected that a killer was about to strike him in bed. The cell doors were never locked. The cells were nine-by-twelve cubicles and there was Jimmy to fear. Jimmy had killed twenty-eight people before going into prison. Colson stated: "I began to long for a cell with a lock on it."

At the Control Room, the chief deputy admonished Colson in the following sobering words: "The important thing for you to remember is that you remember nothing. No one knows this place exits. You will meet some very unusual men here. Don't discuss your business with them and don't ask them about theirs. When you leave here forget you ever met them. You will only know them by their first names anyway. Obey the rules and mind your own business."[9] In this kind of mental environment, the chances of any friendship developing are very slim. While he was in jail, Colson's father died, certainly adding to his grief.

The prison environment in Alabama for Colson was not different than in Maryland. In fact, conditions there were even worse. After he arrived and walked through "a sterile and windowless receiving room," Colson was ordered to strip down. The prison facility held 250 inmates. He observed that nobody smiled. "Stick-like figures of men were drifting aimlessly and slowly in the open area," he noted. No one here walked fast. He was kept in dormitory G and his number was 23226. The de-individualization was complete.

Like in Baltimore, Maryland, Colson was again warned to keep to himself. If he intended to return alive to his wife Patty, he had better not trust anybody. He was to expect some murders. There were many inmates who would suddenly turn violent. He was not to complain. He needed to be prepared for anything. Maxwell prison was little more than a work camp. The formula for survival here was -- "don't get involved."

One day, when Colson walked close to the visiting area, a prison guard (a "hack") barked at him and ordered that he get out of the area. "When night fell," Colson wrote, "the full weight of what it really means to be imprisoned settled upon me. I felt closed in and fearfully alone even though surrounded by forty other men." Colson added: "It was not homesickness which weighed on my heart, but the barrenness all around me, the empty shells of men, the pervasive feeling of despair that, like the stale air, filled the dusty dimly lit dormitory."[10]

An inmate named Jerry one night warned Colson that he was probably in danger of being assassinated. After this information, Colson was tortured not only by the friendlessness of prison life, but also by the imminent and constant fear of death. Because of these circumstances, Colson determined never to forget his prison ordeal and the great need for prisoners to receive some kind of help to establish their identity, dignity, and humanity.

It is no surprise that the worldwide ministry of the Prison Fellowship emerged after Chuck Colson came out of prison. Colson thus fulfilled his late father's dreams for prison reform in the United States. I also believe that the Prison Fellowship has helped to address the problem of friendlessness which Colson experienced while in prison.

## Friendless Runaways And Prostitutes

The need for friendship is not an exclusive problem faced only by foreign students, immigrants and prisoners. Many homeless people, young runaways, and prostitutes have no real friends

*Compassion International* reported in one of its telecasts on March 14, 1996 that about one million young people roam the streets of Brazil's mean and friendless cities every day. Many of these young people end up as prostitutes who are preyed upon by pimps. In the United States, as well as in many large cities of many countries, young homeless people are exploited by people who can hardly be called their friends.

Sister Mary Rose McGeady of Covenant House in New York dedicated her little book, *God's Lost Children* (1991) to the one million "homeless children who slept on America's streets last year, scared, cold, hungry, alone, and most of all, desperate to find someone who cares."[11] Also, McGeady provided the names of fourteen such young homeless people and challenged us all to help.

## Friendless Campuses

As a college professor, I know of many students who are often sad because they are without friends. On many college and university campuses, I have seen such students walk around with long drawn faces, drooping heads and miserable looks. In the classroom, such students sit silent, afraid to answer any questions, and distracted. The fraternities and sororities have capitalized on their miseries. These sororities and fraternities are now centers purporting to provide friendship.

In her wonderful book, *The Friendship of Women*. Dee Brestin recounts her experiences when she was a college student at Northwestern University. Her roommate, in her freshman year, was named Heather and they had become good friends. Heather had cautioned Brestin to choose her friends carefully. In spite of Heather's admonition, Brestin was determined to pledge in a sorority.

She wrote: "So strong was my need for connection, so fearful was I of not being identified with a sorority, that I convinced Heather to go through rush and pledge with me."[12] The sorority accepted her but rejected Heather. She says that she was shocked by the rejection. Brestin represented the multitudes of campus students dying for genuine friends either on the college or university campuses.

## Men Without Friends

Men, too, need friends. Like Dee Brestin, many young men on college campuses are friendless. All around us, there are men without friends. In his path breaking book, James Osterhaus, a practicing psychologist in Fairfax Station, Virginia, flatly states: "Let's get it right out here in the open: most men just plain don't have friends." He disclosed that 33% of Americans surveyed said that they spent less time in 1991 than in the previous year with friends.

Osterhaus cited Leighton Ford, well known among American evangelicals, as saying: "The facts are clear: millions of men are friendless."[13]  Dr. Osterhaus also pointed out that the former Senate chaplain, Dr. Richard Halverson, made friendship a central part of his ministry when he was a pastor at Hollywood Presbyterian Church in southern California. Dr. Halverson understood that many people who attend church and sit week after week in the pews are without friends. Halverson lamented that "fellowship has become a means to an end in our culture, even in the church."[14]

Many, many people have told me over the years that

they are without real friends. A person may be working in a large office or corporation for many years and yet has very few real friends -- or none at all. It is, therefore, not a surprise to me that the need for friends and friendship in America has found outlets in the pen-pal and dating business. Nearly every major newspaper today now provides space for the "PERSONALS."

Hundreds of names of men and women seeking each other for dates are printed in these newspapers week after week. The need for real friends and friendships lies at the root of this booming "market." The internet has added more opportunities to this market. Muriel James and Louis M. Savary, in their book, *The Heart of Friendship*, have amply elaborated on "the needs of friendship."[15] I recommend their book.

## A Nation of Strangers

The weight of material which we have examined leads us to state that America is not a very friendly society which we would like to think or believe that it is. Rather, America is a nation of strangers, as Vance Packard had discovered.

I have actually heard some parents say to their children: "don't talk to strangers," as if strangers are vermin to be dreaded. We have instilled into many young people the feeling of friendlessness, and even an attitude of hostility toward those that we ought to show hospitality to. But Carole King, in a popular song from the sixties or seventies, explained how good it was to know that one had a friend. In a country where the average American moves about fourteen times in his or her lifetime,[16] the need for friends and friendships cannot be overemphasized.

This constant moving from place to place, or "uprootedness" as Packard termed it, has made developing friendships which last a little more difficult to attain. However, it is no excuse for us not to strive to be human and show a real gesture of humanity to those around us. After all, friendship is a sound testimony that we possess a sense of humanity and are willing to share it. The snob does not belong to the world of real friends. And who really needs a snob around? But the presence and smile of a friend are as refreshing as the smell of rose flowers from an early morning breeze.

# CHAPTER TWO

## THE MEANING OF A REAL FRIEND

*A true friend unbosoms freely, advises justly, assists readily, adventures boldly, takes all patiently, defends courageously, and continues a friend unchangeably.*

— William Penn, 1644-1718

There are many people who are unwilling to admit that they have never given any serious thought to what constitutes real friendship. They have not been willing to pay the price for friendship. They have actually, at certain times, been outright unfriendly.

In this book, you will discover that there are many benefits of friendship you were not aware of before. Also, you will know what a real friendship is. As a result, hopefully, you will make developing friendships more of a priority in your life so that you can benefit from having some truly good and valuable friends. You will also become a good friend to others.

So, what, then, is friendship? What are its principles and its characteristics? What qualities should one look out for in the selection or choice of friends? What are the hinderances to a long-lasting friendship? One quick way to answer these questions is to examine what some famous biographers, writers and experts have said about friendship.

For example, Martin Tupper (1810-1889), the English poet and author of *Proverbial Philosophy*, wrote that "A book is the best of friends, the same today and for ever."[1] So, is friendship about our acquisition of and acquaintance with many books? A book can't give you a ride to go pick up your car in the shop. Neither can it bring you a meal when you are sick. A friend can.

We may also have to consider what Jeremy Taylor (1613-1667), the English scholar and Anglican bishop said. "By friendship," Taylor wrote, "you mean the greatest love, the greatest usefulness, the most open communication, the noblest sufferings, the severest truth, the heartiest counsel, and the greatest union of minds of which brave men and women are capable."[2]

Plato believed that "the love of man to woman is a thing common and of course, and at first partakes more of instinct and passion than of choice; but true friendship between man and man is infinite and immortal."[3] Euripides (485 - 406 B.C.) said that "life has no blessing like a prudent friend."[4]

What emerges from this scanning process through the opinions of other reputable writers on friendship is the fact that the list of such writers soon becomes inexhaustible. Besides, we constantly have to stop to analyze what each of these writers meant so as to fully comprehend their ideas about friendship. For instance, Plato's statement quoted above does not tell us too much. Euripides's idea is not a definition of friendship but a pointer to the benefit derivable from friendship. Fortunately, this task of scanning through literature for the meaning of friendship has been dealt with by other persons.

## Perspectives On Friendship

Two such persons are Patricia Dreier in *The Gold of Friendship* (1980) and Hal I. Larson in *You Are My Friend* (1991).[5] I highly recommend these two books. There are also other dictionary compilations which are useful. I have cited two of these in the endnotes. And William J. Bennett, the former U. S. Secretary of Education under the Reagan presidency, has a good section on friendship in his 1993 book on virtues.

I have indicated that it is important to analyze what some writers have said about friendship. In my view, the writings of Marcus Tullius Cicero (106 - 43 B.C.), king Solomon (970 - 931 B.C.),[6] Michel de Montaigne (1533 - 1592), and Clive Staples Lewis (1898-1963), put together, provide a wealth of insights on the meaning and description of friendship.

These four writers also provide us with the do's and don'ts of friendship. For us to fully comprehend what friendship really is, we should turn to the great minds of Cicero, Solomon, Montaigne, and Lewis. But, let me begin with a brief introduction of each of my chosen authors.

Cicero was a Roman author, orator, and statesman who, in his lengthy essay on friendship, boldly declared that only the wise are uniquely qualified to engage in any kind of discourse on this subject. Many centuries before Cicero, the wise King Solomon of ancient Israel provided some insights on the matter of friendship.

In his anthology of wise sayings (known to us as Proverbs), Solomon had no less than twenty-four verse references relating to friends and friendship. Indeed, the entire Bible has, at least, one-hundred and seven such references on the matter of friends, friendliness and friendship. The Bible ,is silent on the matter of friendlessness.

The New Testament book of *St. Luke* alone has fifteen such references. Therefore, one can conclude that the Bible is concerned about human friendship. And, properly understood, the Bible is a book which describes relationships between man and man, and between man and his creator who is deeply interested in friendships.

Michel de Montaigne was a sixteenth century French essayist and thinker. Generally regarded as the father of the modern essay, Montaigne also wrote about friendship. Clive Staples [C. S.] Lewis was a celebrated and distinguished British scholar and atheist. Later, he became this century's greatest Christian apologist and author of *The Four Loves*, a book that examined affection, eros, charity, and friendship. Now that we know who our four celebrated men are, let us turn our attention to Cicero and the other trio.

## Cicero On Friendship

Cicero's essay on this topic is one of the most heart-warming and interesting pieces in Western literature which can cause you to chuckle and smile as you read it. In a letter that he sent to Atticus, his friend, Cicero examined the most remarkable friendship which existed between two people he knew -- Gaius Laelius and Publius Scipio. What Cicero believes and thinks about friendship comes through the lips of Laelius.[7]

Cicero had a definition of friendship when he wrote: "Now friendship may be thus defined: a complete accord on all subjects human and divine, joined with mutual good will and affection."[8] He said that friends are the most valuable and beautiful furniture of life. According to him, friendship had its origin in love, that is, *genuine love*, not in exploitation nor in selfishness.

He observed that the Latin word for friendship -- *amicitia* -- is derived from the same word for love -- *amor*. Therefore, Cicero argued that friendship cannot be based upon weakness nor upon the need for help. "Friendship by its nature admits of no feigning, no pretence." Friendship must both be genuine and spontaneous. It must spring from a natural impulse rather than from a wish for help.

Cicero believed that "when a man's confidence in himself is greatest, when he is so fortified by virtue and wisdom as to want nothing [material] and to feel absolutely self-dependent, it is then that he is most conspicuous for seeking out and keeping up friendships."[9] This kind of friendship is eternal.

In the mind of Cicero, friendship is the greatest thing in the world. He regards the theme of friendship a noble one. The characteristics of friendship, that is, its nature and the rules to be observed, are intimacy, interactiveness, joyfulness, pre-eminence, and permanence. The real secret of friendship lies in the most complete harmony in tastes, pursuits, and in the sentiments of those involved in a particular mode of friendship.

According to Cicero, a cardinal principle to be noted is that "friendship can only exist between good men." By "good," he meant "those actions and lives [which] leave no question as to their honor, purity, equity, and liberality; who are free from greed, lust, and violence; and who have the courage of their convictions."[10]

Cicero found it hard to believe that friendship can be preserved without virtue. He believed that one can eliminate affection from any relationship but "you cannot do so from friendship." Without affection, a relationship may exist in name only, but friendship cannot do so. He contended that life is only worth living when friendship is embraced.

He queried: "What can be more delightful than to have some one to whom you can say everything with the same absolute confidence as to yourself? Is not prosperity robbed of half its value if you have no one to share your joy?" Then he added: "Misfortunes would be hard to bear if there were not some one to feel them even more acutely than yourself."[11]

Picturesquely, Cicero pointed to the emptiness of an affluent life without friends when he asked: "Who, in heaven's name, would choose a life of the greatest wealth and abundance on condition of neither loving or being loved by any creature?" He went on to answer his own question: "That is the sort of life tyrants endure." Such tyrants "can count on no fidelity, no affection, no security for the goodwill of anyone. For them all is suspicion and anxiety; for them [there] is no possibility of friendship. Who can love one whom he fears, or by whom he knows that he is feared?"[12]

The most difficult thing, in Cicero's view, is for a friendship to remain unimpaired to the end of someone's entire life. Many things can bring about such an impairment or disruption: conflict of interests, differences over political opinions, and the frequent changes in one's character. Also, there might arise a spirit of rivalry between partners in a friendship. The most fatal blow to friendship in the majority of cases comes from "the lust of gold." For many politicians, this blow may come in the area of rivalry for office and fame.

Cicero considered that it was immoral for anyone in a friendship relationship to expect his or her friend to be an accessory to a crime or any action that would inflict injury or a wrong. He advised that a clear-cut refusal must be made in such a circumstance. Such demands and expectations are only present in people without scruples. He maintained that one must never be an abettor of such madness. One should never plead that one's wrong actions were performed in the best interests of a friend. This is no valid excuse for a wrong action. A man's virtue, he insisted, is the original cause of any friendship.

Cicero recognized that there were some other theories of friendship with which he disagreed. He identified three such theories:

♦ We should love our friend just as much as we love ourselves, and no more.
♦ Our affection to friends should exactly correspond and equal theirs to us.
♦ A friend should be valued at exactly the same rate as a man values himself.[13]

Cicero's response to the first proposition above is that it holds the view that "our regard for ourselves is to be the measure of our regard for our friend." Cicero argued that this is not always true because there are many things that one would not have done for oneself, but would do for a friend. There are many things which people of upright character would voluntarily forgo so that their friends may be advantaged. Sometimes, we even extend some kindness to undeserving people.

The second theory "limits friendship to an exact equality in mutual good offices and good feelings." Cicero replied that such a theory "reduces friendship to a question of figures in a spirit far too narrow and illiberal." He pointed out that "true friendship appears ... to be something richer and more generous than it receives."[14]

Cicero considered the third theory to be the worst ever proposed, that is, "that a friend's estimate of himself is to be the measure of our estimate of him." He responded by stating that it often happens that a man or woman may have *too little* an estimate of himself or herself. A person may also be lacking proper and adequate self-esteem. Should we therefore adopt such a standard as the rule in our friendship? Certainly not.

Along with this third view is the popular dictum: "You should love your friend with the consciousness that you may one day hate him." This maxim, Cicero warned us, "is the utter destruction of friendship." He asks: "How can a man be friends with another, if he thinks it possible that he may be his enemy?"[15]

The proper rule of conduct is to be careful in the selection of our friends so as to never enter into any kind of friendship with a person whom we could under any circumstances come to hate. And, it ought to be clear to us that the central flaw in the three theories cited above are the ingredients of egocentricity and selfishness.

The real test of a friendship is that "the characters of two friends must be stainless." That is, one should not bring into friendship something which could mar the reputation and integrity of a friend. When we look out for stability and permanence in a friendship, the thing to bear in mind is *loyalty*. Cicero explained that this loyalty does not mean blind loyalty. Rather, it means that there must be the absence of pretence.

There must be transparent honesty between the partners in a friendship. Neither partner in a friendship should dismiss outright any accusations brought against the other concerning any wrongdoing. Nor should either friend jump into unsubstantiated conclusions about the guilt of the other. The best thing to do is to keep an open mind. There must be no open display of superiority.

The process of securing a good friendship must begin with an individual. A person must be good and then look out for another of like character and quality. If one must remonstrate, there must be no bitterness. If one must reprove or correct one's friend, there must be no insults. According to Cicero, if our friend will not listen to our sound words of wisdom and advice, it is best to give him or her up in despair.

The essence of friendship, Cicero reminds us, is that two minds become one. "In the face of a true friend a man sees as it were a second self. So that where his friend is he is; if his friend be rich, he is not poor; though he be weak, his friend's strength is his; and in his friend's life he enjoys a second life after his own is finished."[16]

Cicero pointed out four blessings inherent in any friendship. Friendship:

♦ Gives us bright hopes for the future
♦ Forbids weakness and despair
♦ Brings with it virtue and harmony
♦ Has a binding force between persons in a relationship.

He argued that anyone who denies that these blessings exist should learn from observing the effects of quarrels and feuds which sometimes lead to wars. He laid down the following ten rules on friendship:

♦ Neither ask for nor consent to do what is wrong. "For friendship's sake" is a discreditable plea.

- Ask from friends and do for friends only what is good.
- Do not engage in a friendship solely for the material benefit, which you hope to derive.
- Expect some mental pain from the anxieties that come at the early stages of a friendship.
- Do not let excessive affection hinder the highest interests of your friends.
- It is not so much what one gets from a friend which gives one pleasure as the warmth of his feeling.
- Remember that we only care for a friend's service if it has been prompted by love.
- Friendship does not follow material advantage but the other way around.
- When we break a friendship, it ought to die a natural rather than a violent death. "We should take care that friendship is not converted into active hostility."[17]
- Every friendship must include respect for each other. When respect is gone, "friendship has lost its brightest jewel.... Nature has given us friendship as the handmaid of virtue, not as a partner in guilt."[18]

Cicero concluded his essay with the insistence that *next to virtue, the greatest of all things is friendship.* The tone of his discourse suggests that he placed friendship on a high scale of priority in human experience. In my judgment, Cicero was quite idealistic about some aspects of friendship, raising its standard up to the level of near-perfection. But none of us is perfect. We can only do our very best to retain good friendships.

## Solomon On Friendship

Solomon ben David (King Solomon) is said to have had international reputation for wisdom, although I find it hard to understand what wisdom there was in his surrounding himself with seven hundred wives and three hundred concubines. The Bible states that, in his later years, Solomon's harem of women turned his heart to idolatry.

Nevertheless, Solomon is said to have spoken three thousand proverbs and had one thousand and five songs.[19] If he were alive in America today, he probably would have written enough songs to win him an Oscar or Amy award. Ours is an age in which even a frog can croak and merchandise his lyrics!

Solomon's ideas on friendship are found in the Bible. In the King James's version, the terms used are friend, friends, friendly, and friendship. Sometimes, the translators substitute the word "neighbor" for friend (Prov. 6 : 1; 17 : 18). All the references considered herein are from the book of Proverbs. So, let us examine fourteen references to friendship by Solomon.[20]

1. "The rich hath many friends" (14 : 20). Solomon observes that the admirers of wealthy people are often many. This is a fact of life as the poor are often ignored or shunned.

2. "A whisperer separateth chief friends" (16 : 28). This is an insight into the vicious role of whisperers -- murmurers, slanderers, and gossippers who often destroy close relationships with their tongue.

3. "He that repeateth a matter separateth friends" (17:9).Here Solomon repeats the sentiment expressed in 16 : 28. A person who spreads gossip, or the tale-bearer, cannot promote friendship and love. For example, harping on past faults between spouses has

destroyed many marriages.

4. "A friend loveth at all times" (17: 7). The love of a true friend is constant, especially needful in times of adversity. Solomon here points to the permanence of friendship.

5. "A man that hath friends must shew himself friendly: and there is a friend that sticketh closer than a brother" (18 : 24). Solomon is saying that it is better to have one good, faithful friend than many unreliable ones.

The Ibibios, one the many ethnic groups in Nigeria, say that a good friend is better than a bad brother. In the same way, a really precious friend is much more appreciated than a far-away, good-for-nothing brother. Solomon also admonishes that people who need friends must be friendly themselves.

6. "Wealth maketh many friends" (19 : 4). This sentiment has already been expressed in 14 : 20. It is a fact of life that the rich will attract many friends.

7. "Every man is a friend to him that giveth gifts" (19 : 6). This is a repetition of 19 : 4.

8. "All the brethren of the poor do hate him: how much more do his friends go far from him?" (19 : 7). This is another repetition of 14 : 20. These repetitions by Solomon might be for the sake of emphasis, his indirect way of warning us about the applause that the rich often receive but which is not the proper ground for friendship.

9. "He that loveth pureness of heart, for the grace of his lips the king shall be his friend" (22 : 11). Solomon

believes that one who is honest and gracious in speech will be welcome at the courts of royalty.

10. "Make no friendship with an angry man; and with a furious man thou shalt not go" (22 : 24). Solomon simply says: "Stay away from a hot-tempered man. Do not make friendship with him." The warning is to avoid a hothead who often may act before he thinks or may talk without reflection. This kind of a man will not promote good friendships, but instead will likely bring injury.

11. "Every man shall kiss his lips that giveth a right answer" (24 : 26). Although this does not explicitly refer to friendship, Solomon maintains that a truthful answer is the mark of friendship. Here, he uses the symbolism of a kiss to convey his idea.

In the Middle Eastern world of Persia, kissing on the lips was a sign of friendship. Among the Ibibios, sharing a meal with someone is a sign of friendship. It is clear here also that one may not receive a kiss on the lips unless one is deemed to be a friend.

12. "Faithful are the wounds of a friend; but the kisses of an enemy are deceitful" (27 : 6). This thought buttresses the idea discussed in 24 : 26 that a reprove given out of love is preferable to the insincere and deceptive kisses of an enemy. The world is ever mindful of the kisses from a Judas Iscariot who betrayed his master. The "wounds" of a friend correct rather than hurt.

13. "Ointment and perfume rejoice the heart: so doth the sweetness of a man's friend by hearty counsel" (27 : 9). Simply put, the advice from a true friend is generally pleasant since it is often well intended.

14. "Thine own friend, and thy father's friend, forsake not" (27 : 10). Solomon refers here to that friendship which transcends generational gaps. Its longevity and permanence have some practical benefits. Therefore, he advises us not to cut it loose. One should not forsake old family friends.

It appears here that Solomon is thinking of a community that is in harmony with itself. It is the web of sincere and good friendships, which ties such a community together. Solomon helps us to understand that without friendship in any community, such a community will crumble and will not grow nor prosper. Therefore, the harmony that a community may enjoy depends upon the degree of friendly relations to be found within that community.

It is unfortunate that nowhere does Solomon define what friendship is. I assume that he takes for granted that his audience knows what it is. He offers some useful prescriptions and is emphatic on the roles which money and wealth play in the maintenance or destruction of friendships. His thoughts on this subject are down to earth and practical. We may ignore them if we desire to rush into our peril.

## Montaigne On Friendship

Montaigne's essay *Of Friendship*[21] is written in the sixteenth century grammar and style of his day. His essay is one of the most difficult things I have ever read. This "father" of the modern essay does not make it easy for one to penetrate into his mind, at least, as far as friendship is concerned.

Having said this, I can tell from his writings that Montaigne highly valued friendship. He considered friendships very important in his life. He had known and experienced true friendship with a lad of sixteen who later died and left him emotionally crippled. He found himself in deep sorrow and sadness after his friend's death. He had become so accustomed to being around his friend and "to be never single, that me thinks I am halfe my selfe."[22]

Montaigne identified four kinds of friendships, namely, natural, social, hospitable, and "venerian" love. He did not expatiate on these four categories. But he stated that "friendship is nourished by communication." He regarded admonitions and corrections as "the chiefest offices of friendship."[23] He believed that "friendship is enjoyed according as it is desired, it is neither bred nor nourished, nor increaseth."[24] Here, he seems to have contradicted himself.

Montaigne was right on what he said about the enjoyment of friendship. But I believe that he was wrong about the improvement we may make about our friendship relationships. He wrote that "friendship is enjoyed according as it is desired, it is neither bred, nor nourished, nor increaseth ...." I believe that friendships can grow; they can be nourished and improved upon as the degree of intimacy deepens. If love can grow, so can friendship.

Montaigne disagreed with Cicero's view that one must not collaborate with a friend in wrong-doing. He used the term "yoke" to describe the kind of commitment which ought to exist between friends. But, like Cicero, he believed that friendship must embrace virtue and the "conduct of reason."[25] He used the term "amity" to describe what he considered to be the purest kind of friendship. In this kind of friendship, "a man must march with the bridle of [wisdom] and precaution in his hand."

With Cicero, Montaigne repudiated the kind of friendship which presupposes that we can under any circumstances turn to hate our friends. He called this reasoning "[abominable.]" According to Montaigne, the love we bear in a true friendship is indivisible. He believed that "each man doth so wholly give [himself] unto his friend, that he hath nothing left him to divide else-where."[26]  "A singular and [principal] friendship dissolveth all other duties, and freeth all other obligations."[27]  With a true friend, one's soul "is all and whole enshrinde."[28]

It is difficult to decipher more fully what Montaigne really thought about this subject. He seemed to contradicted himself at times (as in "friendship is nourished by communication") and I believe that some of his ideas bordered on the "yoke" rather than on the freedom that should be inherent in friendship relationships. He reminds me of those "friends" who are hyper-possessive and narcissistic.

## Lewis On Friendship

I ought to emphasize the point that before C. S. Lewis became a Christian, he was a staunch atheist, of the kind of Bertrand Russell, his fellow countryman from England and a world renowned scholar. After his conversion, Lewis gave his energies to writing and public speaking. In his book, *The Four Loves*, he identified four categories of relationships, one of these being friendship.

In order to fully develop his idea of friendship, Lewis placed it in contrast with affection, eros, and charity. According to him, affection (in Greek known as *storge*) is the kind of love between parents, their offspring, and vice-versa. It is the modest fondness we hold for someone or something, like our cats or dogs. It is often closely associated with that which is familiar.[29]

By eros, Lewis meant the state which we call "being in love" or "that kind of love which lovers are 'in'."[30] Lewis took pains to point out that by eros he was not inquiring into the sexuality which is common to all humans and even to animals. But his term does include "the carnal or animal sexual element" which he called *Venus*. *Venus* represents "what is known to be sexual by those who experience it." And, "eros includes other things besides sexual activity." Lewis maintains that "sexuality may operate without eros or as part of eros."[31]

Lewis saw charity in terms of *agape*, the God kind of love. He quoted from I John 4 : 10 -- "God is love" -- to support his exposition on charity. Having made these clarifications and distinctions, Lewis provided us with a brief historical account of the development and characteristics of friendship. Especially useful are his insights on the adverse uses of friendship and "the degrading pleasure of exclusiveness" which the abuse of friendship may engender. Reading Lewis, it is evident that he knew of Cicero's and Aristotle's definitions of friendship.

Lewis lamented that "very few modern people think friendship a love of comparable value at all." In stark contrast to this attitude is that of the ancients who regarded friendship as "the happiest and most fully human of all loves; the crown of life and the school of virtue. The modern world, in comparison, ignores it."

Aristotle saw friendship in terms of *philia*. Cicero, as we have seen, called it *amicitia*. But why does modern society devalue friendship so much? Lewis replied that it is because few people today ever really experience true friendship. Many who regard themselves as being in friendship are either experiencing affection or erotic love.

Lewis contends that "the exaltation of instinct," "the return to nature," and "the exaltation of sentiment" tend to have dealt a death-blow on friendship. Hence, "we can live and breed without friendship." Moreover, those who may engage themselves in real friendships are often open to the charge of being homosexuals, particularly if their relationship is between the sexes -- that is, man to man or woman to woman.

Lewis counters this charge with "those who cannot conceive friendship as a substantive love but only as a disguise or elaboration of eros betray the fact that they have never had a friend." He argues that the homosexuality theory does not seem plausible to him since "kisses, tears and embraces are not in themselves evidence of homosexuality."

For him, the matrix of friendship is companionship. Persons in friendship must have shared interests. True friendship is the least jealous. The partners in a true friendship have a common vision and are drawn together by a belief in the same truth. "The very condition of having friends is that we should want something else besides friends."

Lewis insists that "friendship must be about something. Friendship is in reality a love." Erotic love may lead to friendship between lovers, but erotic love is not necessarily friendship. Erotic kind of friendship will soon fade away -- as quickly as when the objective is satisfied. Underlying an erotic love may be a need to be needed. But true "friendship is utterly free from affection's need to be needed." The role of a benefactor is irrelevant in a real friendship. "Eros will have naked bodies; friendship naked personalities."

Furthermore, Lewis believes that each person in a real friendship comes into it not for what gains he or she might get. Each person is unique and distinctive within the relationship. There is no attempt to manipulate nor use each other. Even gratitude is no enrichment to this virtue. "The mark of perfect friendship is not that help will be given when the pinch comes ... but that, having been given, it makes no difference at all."

The "kingliness of friendship" lies in the fact that "in a circle of true Friends each man is simply what he is: stands for nothing but himself." Friendship is "free from instinct, free from all duties but those which love has freely assumed, almost wholly free from jealousy, and free without qualification from the need to be needed."

Friendship, Lewis asserted, "is eminently spiritual. It is the sort of love one can imagine between angels." This is the kind of love which raises us above humanity, the kind that made the ancients feel that they were catapulted to the realms of the gods or angels.

Lewis observed one particular social benefit which friendship provides. He wrote that friendships always seem to be the basis for the emergence of many closely knit societies and organizations. For instance, "every civilized religion began in a small group of friends." He stated that it is not an accident that the early Quakers called themselves the Society of Friends.

Mathematics began when a few Greek friends got together to talk about numbers, lines, and angles. The Romantic movement began at the instance of Wordsworth's and Coleridge's frequent discussions. So did the other movements like Communism, the Reformation, the Renaissance, and Methodism. But, Lewis also warns us that a real friendship can have several drawbacks and enemies.

In this regard, he points to the distrust by those in authority toward some exclusive groups. There is also the general attitude of the majority of persons outside the circle of close friends. "Every real friendship is a sort of secession, even a rebellion." Those outside its circle are often viewed as "prigs, prudes and humbugs."

On the other hand, those within the circle of a friendship may knowingly or unknowingly reach a position where they are dominated by the pride of being "insiders" (exclusive) and thus lose touch with the voices outside of their circles. "In a good friendship [group] each member often feels humility towards the rest."

Friends can also find themselves in danger of being members of an elite aristocracy solely because they are attached to each other. It is quite possible to develop a "corporate superiority" attitude toward outsiders. This can lead to what Lewis calls "the degrading pleasure of exclusive-ness" which basks "in the moonshine of our collective self-approval."

When this "corporate superiority" acquires political power and a "united front against the have-nots" becomes its principal occupation, then the original circle of friendship dwindles into "a coven of wanglers," that is, people whose sole motive in a friendship group is dubious and selfish. This kind of friendship group thus sinks back again into mere practical companionship. Ultimately, this friendship group fails to save itself but becomes what people call a "mutual admiration society."

Lewis concludes his analysis by emphasizing that friendship is "the instrument by which God reveals to each the beauties of all the others." He exhorts that "we must try to relate the human activities called 'loves' to that Love which is God." Clearly, then, Lewis' concept of friendship has a deeply religious or spiritual connotation.

Writing as a Christian philosopher and apologist, he believed that this spiritual content is what gives friendship its highest value.

We have examined what real friendship is by analyzing the ideas of Cicero, Solomon, Montaigne and Lewis. What do you think? Tomorrow, when you ask someone to be your friend and he or she retorts, "I am already your friend," what will you say to him or her? I hope that you will recommend what you have learned from reading this book.

# CHAPTER THREE

## FRIENDSHIP IN LONELY AMERICA

*The worst solitude is to be destitute of sincere friendship.*
---Francis Bacon, 1561-1626.

The sickness which we know as loneliness is like the sickness of high blood pressure which the medical authorities have referred to as "a silent killer." If not properly checked and treated, both sicknesses can be fatal.

In this chapter, we are dealing with a problem that has been very common, widespread and universal, a problem which knows no racial nor national boundaries, a problem which has grave consequences and implications for the well-being of any individual, family, society, and nation.

Also, we are concerned with the ways which friendships can become the antidote to loneliness or, at least, lessen the problem. We will seek to understand the importance of friendship in a lonely culture. For, if friendship is what we have understood it to be (see chapter two), then it should have a positive impact or effect upon any lonely individual, society or nation that embraces it. This is what I believe.

And I do not believe that I am being naive or idealistic. I am thinking of friendship, not in the common sense manner, but as a revolutionary idea, and in the same way that Joel D. Block and Diane Greenberg considered it. We should not forget that they believed that friendship's impact upon a man and his spouse and upon the home would be revolutionary.

## Literature On Loneliness

In the last two decades, the problem of loneliness has received greater attention in the United States than ever before. In 1976, the year that Jimmy Carter ran for the presidency, Suzanne Gordon published her popular book, *Lonely In America.* Ten years later, Louise Bernikow of the *New York Times*, released *Alone In America: The Search For Companionship.* In 1996, Jacqueline Olds, Richard S. Schwartz, and Harriet Webster co-authored and published *Overcoming Loneliness In Everyday Life.*[1]

Research in these three publications indicate that the problem of loneliness has not gone away. There have also been several other interesting books on the topic which have appeared since 1976 other than the ones just mentioned. One can readily think of Harold C. Warlick, Jr., *Conquering Loneliness* (1979) and Tim Hansel, *Through the Wilderness of Loneliness* (1991). Even before 1976, there were several published warnings about the anguish of loneliness.

For example, we can point to Philip Slater's, *The Pursuit of Loneliness: American Culture At The Breaking Point* (1970). This was a book which warned a stranger what life in America had become and why. Slater's subtitle suggested that loneliness in the American culture had reached its breaking point. Slater was re-echoing the voice of David Riesman in *The Lonely Crowd: A Study of the Changing American Character* published in 1966, twenty years before Bernikow's book.[2]

Between 1966 and 1986, not less than six other books appeared dealing with the subject of loneliness. The fifteen authors whose books appeared between Slater and Bernikow took the problem of loneliness seriously. We should also do the same. We should remember that in the 1940s, the noted American author, John Gunther, referred to loneliness as "one of the supreme American problems."[3]

In August of 1986, Billy Graham referred to loneliness as "one of the great problems facing Americans today."[4] The great sociological landscapes of our world's large cities constitute wastelands of loneliness – deserts or wildernesses of loneliness.[5] Loneliness is a cankerworm that spares few in America.

## A Typical Scenario

John Doe is single and an evangelist who does his work with zeal, compassion, and dedication. Many nights, he has returned from his evangelistic crusade meetings lonely and depressed. Although the meetings were successful, the singing by the choirs was wonderful, and the people embraced his messages warmly, he came home each night to a dark, empty apartment where King Loneliness stood at the door and greeted him.

At first, John Doe could not understand his feelings. "Preachers were not supposed to be lonely," he murmured to himself. Really? But, now his experience was beginning to bother him. He wonders whether he should get married or "cast out those nagging demons" of loneliness in order to find relief. But who said that marriage would cure his loneliness?

John Doe wonders out aloud: "Am I merely being alone or am I really lonely?" "Who cares?" he sighs and slumps into his bed. He knows that he is uncomfortable with his feelings. He knows that he desperately needs a warm hand to clasp into his and pray and praise God when he returns from those nightly meetings.

John Doe needs someone right there at the door to welcome him home -- someone with whom to share the news of the blessings from his outreach ministry. He needs someone in the flesh, some human being. There is no such thing as having fun when you are lonely and depressed. Loneliness could drive John Doe crazy.

Although *being alone* is not necessarily the same as experiencing loneliness, being constantly and unnecessarily alone, feeling alone, and living a life of aloneness is not the best thing for us social animals. We are created for community life. And his theology notwithstanding, John Doe knows this fact very well. He is certainly not the single-and-happily-enjoying-it type.

John Doe is not unique in his dilemma. Believe me, even married preachers and travelling evangelists do get very lonely. Haven't you ever heard of the preacher who eloped with the choir pianist? What do you think was at the root of that experience? The successful menace of demons of loneliness? Married couples do get lonely too. If you do not believe this, then read Dan Kiley's book, *Living Together, Feeling Alone: Healing Your Hidden*

*Loneliness* (1989), where this matter has been elaborated upon.[6]

Even top managers and CEOs of great corporations, what the popular American radio preacher Charles Swindoll calls "top dogs," do get lonely. Again, what do you think is the cause of some office romances and affairs? You got the answer. Some cases may be due to true friendship and love. But some others are due to loneliness and the need or desire to cure it. Many students and college or university professors are also lonely. Nightclub enthusiasts and frequenters get lonely, too. In short, everyone gets lonely, sometimes.

It is, therefore, not a surprise that David Riesman, the University of Chicago professor, addressed a 386-page book to the lonely crowd of America. Because loneliness affects just about everyone, including the so-called happy-go-lucky person, we must consider pursuing friendship as an alternative response to loneliness.[7] But, what really is this loneliness? Is there any definition for it? Let us examine this matter.

## Meaning of Loneliness

Twenty years ago, Suzanne Gordon simply stated in her book, *Lonely In America*, that loneliness is "an empty feeling ... empty and desolate.[8] She seems to have had difficulty in defining the term. So, she described it as something which includes the feelings of hopelessness, the fear of experiencing loneliness, a desire to deny that one is lonely, and feelings of worthlessness.[9]

Gordon examined the "geography" and experiences of loneliness and devoted half the pages of her book to a discussion of such experiences.[10] The other half of her book was devoted to the analysis of "the loneliness business." She believed that loneliness is contagious.[11]

On her part, when author Louise Bernikow examined male and female loneliness (see chapters three and four of her book) ten years later, she described America as a desert of loneliness, with some oases.[12]   She confessed that at first she thought she knew what loneliness was -- that it belonged to the world of losers.   During her research, however, she "came to find loneliness more and more among people we like to think of as winners."[13]

Bernikow wrote: "People told me they were lonely in offices full of people, in marriages, hanging around on street corners with gangs of alleged friends."[14] She referred to loneliness as a "disease" and reported that there were over nineteen million people living alone in America at the time of her writing. Seven and a half million American men lived by themselves.

That was in 1986.  In 1996, Ruth Westheimer (Dr. Ruth) tells us that 14.2 million women and 9.4 million men live alone in America. While it cannot be said that all these people are loners, could something be wrong with a society where more than twenty-three million people choose or may be forced to live alone?

Bernikow stated that, "Lonely means 'nobody cares about me' often enough, a lack of relatedness to other people, feeling shut out. It sometimes means wanting a mate or it means being married and having no friends. Many people use the word to describe a feeling of being adrift in the universe, atomized, living in a world that comprises only the self."[15]

In their book, *In Search of Intimacy* (1982), Carin Rubenstein and Philip Shaver say that, "loneliness is a healthy hunger for *intimacy* and *community* -- a natural sign that we are lacking companionship, closeness, and a meaningful place in the world."[16] They write that it is "astonishingly difficult" to say exactly what loneliness is without being subjective. But they add that loneliness is a feeling which includes one or more of the following elements: being unattached, feeling the need for friends, experiencing forced isolation, and dislocation.[17]

Dan Kiley studied one hundred cases of "Living Together Loneliness" (LTL) which affects married couples. The "uncoupled loneliness" is the kind most familiar to many of us. But Kiley said that the LTL woman profile includes isolation, bewilderment, agitation, depression, and exhaustion.[18] He added that the college educated, professionally competent, and mothers are the sort of women who suffer from LTL. He warned that loneliness can kill.[19]

Harold C. Warlick, Jr. insisted that loneliness is not the same thing as aloneness, a fact which many experts on the subject agree on. But Warlick added: "Loneliness is the result of lack of *purposeful* activity and lack of relationships."[20] More recently, Tim Hansel has metaphorically stated that "loneliness is like a caterpillar in a cocoon."

Tim Hansel says that, "loneliness is a wrinkled and unappreciated feeling ... like a well-worn pair of faded jeans. It's the kind of feeling you find in the corner of the closet when you're not even looking for it. A leftover ache, rumpled in the corner -- which somehow manages to penetrate your whole being." He adds that "loneliness is not a time of abandonment."[21]

I have drawn from six different sources to show what loneliness is. These sources seem to view loneliness in a negative light. There are others like Clark E. Moustakas, Elisabeth Elliot, and even Tim Hansel who believe that loneliness may have a positive side, with creative and rewarding benefits. These authors belong to the school of thought which sees aloneness or solitude as a good thing.

It is in this sense that Clark Moustakas writes that loneliness "is a force within, a struggle to maintain one's integrity and wholeness in the face of indifference, unresponsiveness, manipulation, and meaningless communication."[22] Hence, Hansel writes that "loneliness need not be an enemy ... it can be a friend.... Loneliness need not be a problem ... it can be an opportunity."[23]

## Three Giants Who Faced Loneliness

Let me share with you some specific examples of very successful people who faced loneliness in their lives. They were all giants in their respective fields. Just knowing that they faced this problem may encourage you not to be daunted by it.

Have you ever heard of Dag Hammarskjold (1905-1961)? He was a Swedish diplomat who became the second Secretary-General of the United Nations Organization (UNO) in 1953. He knew something about loneliness. In his book, *Markings*, he wrote that, "Every deed and every relationship is surrounded by an atmosphere of silence.

Friendship needs no words -- it is solitude delivered from the anguish of loneliness." He went on to admonish: "Pray that your loneliness may spur you into finding something to live for, great enough to die for."[24] These words were penned between 1950 and 1952.

A handsome, deeply religious, and political economist, Hammarskjold had remained unmarried for so many years. His father had been a workaholic who often left his mother alone and lonely. Therefore, Hammarskjold grew up afraid to marry, for fear of subjecting another woman to the same kind of experience which his mother had endured. His problem was compounded by the fact that he was still a bachelor while virtually all of his friends had married.

Between 1950 and 1952, Hammarskjold was terribly frustrated and lonely to the point that once, in late 1952, he even contemplated suicide.[25] The themes of sacrifice and death predominated his diary entries. "He was a very lonely man ... even with his Swedish friends."[26] He himself wrote: "What makes loneliness an anguish is not that I have no one to share my burden, but this: I have only my burden to bear."[27] As with many loners, Hammarskjold found solace from loneliness in his work and deeper dedication.[28]

Reflecting upon his attitude, Hammarskjold said that "work is an anesthetic against loneliness."[29] One of his biographers points out that, in all of his loneliness, Hammarskjold was never a homosexual. This dedicated public servant tragically died in a plane crash in 1961 in Africa. The circumstances of the plane crash still remains a mystery to this day.

Few Americans today know of Samuel Taliaferro Rayburn (1882-1961), the U.S. Congressman who held the office of Speaker of the House of Representatives longer than anyone else in American history. Although he had a successful political career, he was a lonely man. Dr. James Osterhaus writes that "Sam Rayburn was also a man alone."

Born in Texas into a large but poor family, Sam Rayburn could hardly make it through high school because of the poverty of his parents. But he was determined to go to college and dreamed great dreams. Later he ran for state offices in Texas and went on to become the Speaker of the U.S. House of Representatives. He was one of the most powerful public servants in

Washington, D.C. The Rayburn Senate Office Building on Capitol Hill is today named after him.

However, in his private life, Rayburn was frustrated and lonely. "When he was honest with himself, he would confess that the one thing he wanted most was close relationships."[30] His marriage to a very beautiful woman lasted for only three months. Most people in Washington feared him. He had power and influence but not many real and close friends.

Nnamdi Azikiwe (1904-1996) arrived in the United States from Nigeria around 1926, in the heydays of Jim Crow, to study at Storer College in Harper's Ferry, West Virginia. Upon completion of his studies there, he went on to receive a B.A. (1930) and M.A. (1932), both from Lincoln University in Pennsylvania, and another M.Sc. degree in 1933 from the University of Pennsylvania.

Azikiwe then returned to Nigeria, his homeland, to become a journalist, author, politician, and Africa's most popular leader. Between 1953 and 1960, he was the Premier of the defunct Eastern Region, the Governor-General of the new independent state of Nigeria, and the first president when the country became a Republic in 1963.

What is not generally known is that, like other great figures, Azikiwe suffered from loneliness and was even suicidal after finding out that he was starving and without money to buy food and provide himself a shelter in the United States, "God's own country."[31]

Azikiwe personally experienced "the harsh realities of American capitalism and the demeaning aspects of American culture -- racism.... On a particular lonely night, jobless and dejected, after his frustrations in a Pittsburg coal mine, Zik threw himself across the railroad in the face of an approaching train, hoping to end it all by committing suicide."[32] He was rescued by an unknown good samaritan.

By these three examples, we find that students, politicians, and even diplomats can be lonely and suffer from "the ache of loneliness."[33] Rubenstein and Shaver believe that "the only lasting remedies for loneliness are mutual affection and participation in a genuine community."[34]

And, quite frankly, I do not believe that loneliness is a positive experience, or why then would I recommend friendship as an alternative response? I do not believe that loneliness and friendship are synonymous. This is why in 1990, when I published my book, *A Walk Through the Wilderness*, I clearly stated what I meant by loneliness as follows:

> *Loneliness is having a set of persons around you who are basically autonomous, individualistic, and inward looking; and so you cannot call them.*

> *Loneliness is having a set of persons around you who are constantly threatened by vulnerability, openness, and by the need for self-sacrificing concern for others. For these sort of people, concern for our fellowman is equated with socialism.*

> *Loneliness is having a lot of persons around you for whom free and frequent contact is impossible. It is living in an apartment complex with lots of people, none of whom cares what happens to the neighbor next door.*

> *Loneliness is knowing many people, none of*

*whom you may freely and frequently call by phone or even visit without a previous appointment, because they would be bothered by such visits and calls. They would complain that you have violated their "freedom" and privacy. In America, generally, you do not call up a person very early on Saturday mornings.*

*Loneliness is experiencing an inward emptiness and a deeper desire to be wanted, needed, loved, appreciated, and yet having no one upon whom you can honestly lavish your affection.*[35]

All of the above statements describing what loneliness is must be understood within the context of American cultural life. In Nigeria, for example, certain things would not apply because, when I was growing up, I observed that the Ibibio social philosophy is that one must be his brother's keeper. In the United States, the social philosophy is rooted in rugged individualism and the sanctity of property rights.

Americans find it hard to accept the enormous cost and reality of loneliness because, as James Lynch lamentedly put it, "We live in a society in which King Loneliness has no clothing, yet, because everyone believes he is the only one who feels lonely, we tell ourselves that loneliness must be a mirage."[36] Lynch called this kind of denial "the cultural pact of ignorance," and "a peculiar type of conspiracy."

## The Cost of Loneliness

In terms of its emotional, psychological, mental, and

physical impact, the cost of loneliness may never be fully quantified or determined. However, many experts in psychiatry and psycho-therapy agree that loneliness has significant adverse effects on us. James Lynch, in his book, *The Broken Heart: The Medical Consequences of Loneliness* (1972) showed that loneliness can cause many physical problems.

Rubenstein and Shaver wrote that "Loneliness is one of the most pressing and excruciating problems connected with divorce" and that "divorce is the most important cause of adult loneliness in America."[37] Lynch and Earl A. Grollman both agreed that extreme cases of loneliness can lead to suicide. Each year in the United States, 25,000 persons reportedly partake in "self-execution."[38]

Dan Kiley writes that, "Loneliness is an uncontrolled stress."[39] There are few of us who would enjoy being stressed out all the time. In a chapter titled "Loneliness and Health," Rubenstein and Shaver provided a long list of psychosomatic problems associated with loneliness."[40]

Some other known problems related to loneliness include:

♦ violent anger arising from lack of self-esteem
♦ self-blame, bitterness, and resentment
♦ weight problems
♦ substance abuse (e.g. alcohol, drugs, smoking, etc.)
♦ monophobia (alienation and fear of aloneness)
♦ sexual indiscretions (e.g. adultery, prostitution, etc.)
♦ solitary TV addiction leading to loss of useful time and productivity
♦ disillusionment
♦ shop-aholicism (that is, addiction to shopping until you drop dead)
♦ broken hearts and dreams

♦ powerlessness and self-pity

♦ destruction of community by criminal activity

Anyone who still defends loneliness as having a positive side should re-think through the above list.

## Friendship: Antidote For Loneliness

To begin to consider the role which friendship can play in combating loneliness, I suggest that you re-read Chapter Two of this book. It is important to always bear in mind what I mean by friendship. You may even reconsider the issues which I raise in chapters four and five when I examine male and female friendships, respectively.

For women, I recommend that they get a copy of Janice G. Raymond's book, *A Passion for Friends: Toward a Philosophy of Female Affection*, which presents a comprehensive analysis of female friendships. Her "Notes" are particularly helpful.[41] She persuasively treats the "vision" of friendship. Nearly all the people connected with counseling and similar services agree that friendship is the best antidote for loneliness.

Suzanne Gordon, in her concluding chapter, writes that the answer to loneliness is in "the creation of more and better relationships" and not in "exclusive relationships."[42] Rubenstein and Shaver believe that "intimacy and friendship are sources of health; they prolong life."[43] They recommend "social action" which involves calling a friend often or, better still, visiting someone on a regular basis.

Julie Keene and Ione Jensen, who co-authored *Women Alone* in 1995, recommend that any woman living alone should "invite your closest friends to your home to discuss common issues."[44] Earl Grollman insists upon community action. Harold Warlick, Jr., writing from a minister's perspective, counsels the loner to turn to spiritual rejuvenation. Judith Viorst flatly states that "our intimate friendships shelter us from loneliness."[45]

In my book, *A Walk Through The Wilderness* published in 1990, I argued that no healthy person would want to be lonely all the time. We do not always go out looking for loneliness. Often, the anguish is suddenly thrust upon us by external circumstances. And, sometimes, we unconsciously plunge ourselves into situations which lead to loneliness. But the real problem is with *how* to handle this affliction so that we do not end up in a pit of depression or even kill ourselves. We must keep our guard against any actions and tendencies which lead to the doors of King Loneliness.

Therefore, I propose that we strengthen our already existing relationships by doing those things which enhance friendships. We must begin with our minds and re-educate ourselves to realize that no life is a bed of roses. We must re-consider the things which are most important in human life. We must *exalt* personhood, family and close relationships above the mundane and material things, property, fame, and power. We must make time to be with our friends.

Above all, we must always bear in mind that friendships deal with people -- human beings and not with "things." If people and their well-being are more important to us as a way of life than our pursuit of happiness, then we will discover that true friendships bring about happiness and not the other way around.

A simple action of getting to know who your neighbors are instead of pretending that they do not exist, or that they are unimportant because you do not need them at the time, may lead to the beginning of a fruitful and lasting friendship.

Also, when you are in a bus, train or airplane, remember that it is not criminal to smile at the man or woman next to you and to extend a handshake or exchange greetings. You may find out that he or she may be the savior you have been looking for. It is amazing how we have collectively ceased to be friendly by being uncivil in our so-called civilized society.

At the workplace, friendships can be established through the promotion of some outdoor "corporate" activities like tennis, biking, philanthropic interests, and support of community projects. Although some of these activities are in place, heads of corporations should endeavor to make them more meaningful

Thus, our friendships will serve as the antidote for loneliness or, at the least, aid in ameliorating its impact upon our lives. My hope is that you will refuse to embrace King Loneliness but instead seek the warm embraces and kisses of true friendships wherever such may be found. They are closer to you than you may imagine.

## CHAPTER FOUR

---

# WOMAN-TO-WOMAN
# FRIENDSHIP

---

*Please do not ask me to leave you; wherever you go I will go,
and where you stay, I will stay. Your people will be my
people, and your God my God. I want to be buried where
you are buried when you die. May God punish me if
anything other than death parts us.*[1]

> --- Ruth to Naomi   (Ruth 1: 16 -17)

"Female friendship has been one of the best-kept secrets of our society."[2]  So wrote psychologist Dr. Joel D. Block and freelance journalist Diane Greenberg in 1985 in their pioneering work, *Women & Friendship*.  Not entirely true.

When we look at female friendships with the eyes of a historian, we discover that women, of all ages and in all walks of life, have always had friendship relationships among themselves and that such friendships can hardly be described as secret. Indeed, it is hard to hide any genuine friendship.

Psychotherapists Luise Eichenbaum and Susie Orbach, who both founded the Women's Therapy Center Institute in New York and the Women's Therapy Center in London, had been friends for over sixteen years before they co-authored and published their book, *Between Women*, in 1987. Eichenbaum was nineteen and Orbach twenty-five at the time.

They wrote: "We had the air of free women about ourselves. We were full of the headiness of the early days of feminism and we involved ourselves in projects that would benefit women. We spent much time with other women learning and developing the new field of women's studies, discovering together a new way to see our personal histories and challenging our reflexive responses to everything. With a sense of risk and excitement, we gave our female friendships priority."[3]

This sort of admission and activism by Eichenbaum and Orbach hardly supports the notion of the pervasive and secret female friendships. We cannot even claim that this kind of admission and activism is merely recent. In fact, on the contrary, Block and Greenberg discovered in their investigations and research that "women have [had] a rich heritage of friendship that is older than the civilizations of Greece and Rome."[4]

Their book was a celebration of "women's unique bonding as friends."[5] In 1995, in her novel-style writing, Lois Wyse flatly asserted that "women make the best friends,"[6] without proving her point. Wyse's was also "a celebration" book.

I have already hinted that female friendships have a

historical record. Block and Greenberg found out that female friendships did exist in classical, medieval, and Western literature, even though such friendships were often portrayed in distressing and negative terms.[7] Female friendships were clearly depicted in the letters, diaries, and books written by the women themselves. Such women include Carroll Smith-Rosenberg, Mary Wollstonecraft, Angelina and Sarah Grimke, and Mary Church Terrell, to name just a few.

Although Block and Greenberg contend that the Bible has "no hymns to females as friends, only as wives, mothers, and devotees of the Lord," nevertheless it is in the Bible that we find one of the most wonderful and majestic expressions of a woman to woman friendship -- the friendship story of Ruth and Naomi. Block and Greenberg characterized the basis of the Ruth-Naomi relationship as familial rather than friendship. I object to this characterization.

First, as we saw in the previous chapters, the prelude to any love relationship is friendship, whatever its kind, and "the love that includes friendship is the strongest love of all."[8] Familial relationships are supposed to be based upon love and so also upon friendship. Their intensity and quality are no less simply because the friendship revolves around members of a family.

Second, Block and Greenberg tend to miss the essence of biblically-biased relationships. The center of such relationships is God, not man. The honor and glory of such relationships are not man-directed but God-ward. As I will show in chapter five, Jonathan and David were friends, with God at the center of their relationship.

Many modern men and women want relationships which are self-satisfying, God-dishonoring, and downright selfish. Therefore, when we come to examine the story of Ruth and Naomi as an example of true friendship, the essence of the biblical message must be kept in mind. A secular perspective will not do.

## Ruth's Profile

Her name was Ruth Mahlon, described by author Edith Deen as "one of the most lovable women in the Bible."[9] She was a young, attractive Moabitess living east of the Dead Sea in ancient Palestine. Her name appears in literature about thirteen centuries before Christ. The Moabites were the descendants of Abraham's nephew, Lot, who had sex with his own daughters during a drinking stupor after the destruction of Sodom and Gomorrah.

Ruth had married a young Hebrew immigrant to Moab, her country. Her husband, Mahlon, had arrived with his family -- his father, Elimelech, his mother, Naomi, and a brother, Chilion who also had married another Moabitess named Orpah. [Oprah is derived from this name.] The Elimelech family had escaped a famine which was ravaging the city of Bethlehem in the country of Judah at the time.

For ten years after their move, everything seemed to have gone alright. But, soon, tragedy struck the family. Elimelech died and his passing away was followed by the deaths of Mahlon and Chilion. Ruth, Naomi, and Orpah were all left widows.

In time, Naomi received word that the famine in Bethlehem had ceased. She decided to return home. But, before she did, she released her daughters-in-law and persuaded them to return to their parents. Orpah decided to return to her people "but Ruth clung to [Naomi]. Ruth was determined and willing to face an uncertain future in a foreign country." She traveled back with Naomi. Her "most wonderful confession of love ever spoken by a daughter-in-law,"[10] is presented at the beginning of this chapter.

The journey back to Bethlehem was less than 120 miles. Ruth and Naomi arrived at about the beginning of the harvest season for wheat and barley. A dutiful and goal-oriented woman, not used to laziness, Ruth promptly went to work, performing "the lowliest of tasks, that of following the reapers and gathering up the fragments of grain which fell and were left behind for the poor."[11]

Providentially, she was led to the field of one Boaz, a relative of her deceased father-in-law, and a wealthy agriculturalist. Boaz immediately noticed her among his other female harvesters. Her beauty and disposition to hard work may have been the causes for Boaz's quick attention. It may have been love at first sight. It may have been the fact that Ruth was a stranger working among Hebrew women.

But, whatever reason it was, Ruth soon learned that her kindness toward her mother-in-law was no longer a secret in Bethlehem. News of her kindness had gone ahead of her and reached the ears of Boaz even before he discovered her in his field.

Ruth did not thrust herself immediately upon Boaz, even though she was attracted to him and knew that he was her late father-in-law's rich kinsman. She continued to perform her tasks with a humble, quiet, and beautiful spirit. Thus, she became the breadwinner for the old and weary Naomi.

She was definitely a very attractive woman. In her book, *All Of The Women Of The Bible* (1988), Edith Deen has Irving Fineman say that Ruth possessed a "radiant beauty of face and form [which] neither the shadows nor the sad state of her raiment could obscure."[12] Fineman believed that Ruth had gleaming, golden hair and dark eyes. Again, Deen cites another author, Frank Slaughter, as saying that Ruth was "startlingly beautiful, with dark red hair, high cheekbones, and warm eyes." She was like a woman clothed in the "clinging robe of a temple priestess."[13]

If these descriptions of Ruth's physical appearance are correct, it is no wonder that she caught the eyes (and perhaps, the heart) of the much older Boaz, who probably had remained a bachelor up to that time. We are not told that he had a wife. In the course of time, through the wise advice and direction of Naomi, Ruth made a bold, yet humble advance toward Boaz. She must have been charming and extremely irresistible that night when she washed and perfumed herself, and under the silhouette of sunset, she appeared before Boaz in her best dress at his tent in the field.

Boaz was flabbergasted that she was attracted to him. He said to her: "this kindness is greater than that which you have showed earlier. You have not run after the younger men, whether rich or poor" (Ruth 3: 10). He promised to protect her reputation, for she was "a woman of noble character" (3: 11). She would also be protected from any other male suitors who might trouble her. After all, she was merely a gentile, a poor foreigner.

This romance between Ruth and Boaz ended in matrimony. Ruth was remarried to a mighty man of wealth, an elite. She became the mother of Obed and the grandmother of David, the greatest king that Israel ever had. Her name is immortalized in the ancestry of Jesus Christ.

## Naomi's Profile

As we have seen, Naomi's life and story are intricately tied to Ruth's love and friendship. Ruth is the principal heroine and Naomi is the object of Ruth's devotion and love. After her husband and two sons died, Naomi was forlorn and bitter. Formerly a pleasant woman (her name meant pleasant), Naomi now wanted to be known as *mara* (bitter).

She must have been so distraught upon her arrival in Bethlehem that her friends exclaimed: "Can this be Naomi?" Her physical and psychological changes had become so apparent that they caused the exclamation of surprise by her former friends and neighbors.

Definitely, Naomi had changed since her earlier days in Bethlehem. Her social standing or status had changed. She was now a poor widow who had lost both a husband and two sons in a foreign country. At a time when the birth of children and, particularly, sons were expected of a married woman, it was a terrible loss for her. She had ran away to escape poverty but had returned empty-handed and humiliated.

Notwithstanding all these setbacks, Naomi still could be commended for much. It is evident that she had much affection for her family members, particularly, for her daughters-in-law. She was a woman of consideration and fair-mindedness who would not want her daughters-in-law to be burdened by the grievousness of a new environment. Therefore, she urged them to return to their people and to find new life for themselves.

Like Ruth, Naomi was quite unselfish. There is no record that she tried to use or exploit Ruth. Many an immigrant today knows something of the exploitation and abuse when one goes into another country to sojourn. Not so with Naomi Elimelech. In fact, after Ruth gave birth to Obed, we read that Naomi was quite willing to serve as the new baby's nurse.

In Naomi, we see no hint of envy, jealousy, and the competition that is so common in people today. Obed was practically Naomi's grandson. She rejoiced to see Ruth marry Boaz. The harmony between the two women was such that Naomi's neighbors remarked: "Thy daughter-in-law, which loveth thee, ... is better to thee than seven sons" (4:15). Obviously, Naomi was lovable in order to deserve this compliment.

## Their Bond of Friendship

We should now consider what was responsible for the sustenance of this kind of friendship. There are many things which can be observed. First among them is the character of Ruth. After arriving in Bethlehem, Ruth was popularly known as "a virtuous woman" -- a woman of noble character. The distinctive qualities of such a woman are outlined in Proverbs 31:10-31. It is difficult not to fall in love and befriend such a woman.

Second, Ruth was a determined loyalist, the type of a friend who sticks closer than a brother or sister, a woman who could not be easily persuaded to take the path of least resistance. We must keep in mind that *she did not have to return to Bethlehem with Naomi.* Orpah, her sister-in-law, made a choice which was equally open to Ruth.

No one would have blamed her for acting exactly like Orpah. It was the reasonable thing to do. But love is not always reasonable. I have often said that when two people fall in love, they do "crazy" things. Ruth was committed to a kind of faithfulness which never goes unrewarded.

She had come under the wings of the Lord God of Israel, to trust and seek refuge in Him. She couldn't be disappointed!

Third, Ruth was an intelligent, humble, and obedient woman. When she first met Boaz, she did not thrust herself upon him because he was rich. When Boaz treated her kindly, Ruth's reaction was surprise with a gentle spirit of humility. She bowed herself to the ground. She was not pompous and proud because she was attractive. Rather, she deemed herself less favored than the servant girls of Boaz (2:13).

Ruth would have gladly contented herself with the role and status which her new environment offered her. Such humility is often rewarded. When Naomi instructed her on what to do to gain Boaz's favor in the direction of matrimony, she obeyed. Implicitly, she trusted the mature judgment of her mother-in-law. There is nothing here of the self-willed, haughty, and hot-headedness many people possess in our modern times. This character trait in Ruth undoubtedly aided their friendship to function harmoniously.

Fourth, Ruth was a very caring person. The biographer of this story, which Goethe called "the loveliest little idyll that tradition has transmitted to us,"[14] takes care to point out that after Ruth had eaten at Boaz's field, she carried home the left-over, the ready-made food for Naomi. She wanted her mother-in-law to taste of the same stuff she had eaten from Boaz. What a sharing friend! Tight-fisted misers never make good friends.

By now we should realize that the friendship which existed between Ruth and Naomi was one which was solidly rooted in genuine love. Of this love, Edith Deen says that, "Love had worked the miracle in Ruth's life. She was beloved by all because she was so lovable. She had proved that love can lift one out of poverty and obscurity, love can bring forth a wonderful child, love can shed its rays, like sunlight, on all whom it touches, even a forlorn and weary mother-inlaw. Ruth's love had even penetrated the barriers of race."[15]

At once, we must notice that this female friendship between Ruth and Naomi was one which cut across ethnicity and racial boundaries. Ruth was a gentile and Naomi a Hebrew. The friendship also cut across national and cultural lines, a foreshadowing of the kind of friendship which led Jesus Christ to visit the despised region of Samaria and to speak to a "low-life" Samaritan woman.

I need to stress the point that Ruth and Naomi were from different ethnic, national, and cultural backgrounds but love hooked them up together in a solid bond of friendship. How many of us have international friends? How many of us have friends of different ethnic and cultural backgrounds? I ask these questions because I reside in the United States where prejudice against immigrants is on the rise. This is a country with a long-lasting problem of racism.

In Africa recently, ethnic rivalries and animosities have led to genocides and blood-baths, like in Rwanda and Burundi. There is an urgent need to teach people that they can have friends across ethnic and racial or even national boundaries. I shall return to this matter in chapters nine and ten.

The Ruth-Naomi friendship, like the Jonathan-David relationship, also bridged the generational gap. Naomi was definitely older than Ruth. The two women came from different generational backgrounds. But it did not matter at all. I believe that Ruth learned a lot of things which came from her years of experiences and derived much wisdom from the advice which Naomi provided her with.

If today's women make the best friends, as Lois Wyse has contended, then it is important that solid friendships between the older women and the younger ones be encouraged. Our young people seem to be increasingly aimless and without much wisdom. They are perishing because of foolishness. Solid friendships with older women could have kept the younger ones from doing some foolish things they have done. And the society would profit from these kinds of relationships. Scripture teaches that the older women should teach the younger ones.

I am not suggesting that young women should eternally be yoked to and dependent upon older women. Rather, as Marjory Z. Bankson has shown, young women can benefit from the kind of interdependence which Ruth and Naomi had. For instance, Bankson writes that Ruth's courage "stirred Naomi out of wintry silence."[16] I am affirming that the myth of self-sufficiency has no room in a world that is desperately in need of the assistance which one can derive from solid friendships.

This point of view is the central thesis in the book by Eichenbaum and Orbach which I mentioned earlier. Traditionally, it had been believed that female friendships were often marred by feelings of envy, competition, and anger. Eichenbaum and Orbach passionately denied that this was so. They argued that having been trained from an early age to be nurturers and care-givers, most women grow up to attach themselves with one another with sensitivity, caring, and empathy.

Eichenbaum and Orbach insisted that "connectedness, attachment, affiliation and selflessness have been and still are largely the foundations of women's experience. A woman knows herself and gathers a sense of well-being through her connection and attachment to others."[17] Like Ruth and Naomi, we do need to learn how to lean on one another in times of troubles. But even if our lives were trouble-free, we would still need one another in order to motivate, encourage, and applaud the successes of our friends.

Eichenbaum and Orbach also stated that, "Because women derive so much of their identity and a sense of well-being through attachment, and because women's friendships contain a merged attachment, a friend with whom one has made a significant attachment serves almost as a part of the self." They added: "The sharing of time, activities, aspirations, pleasures, and pains transforms an individual sense of inner emptiness into one of rootedness and connectedness."[18]

Some men may react to all this with suspicion that what Eichenbaum and Orbach have maintained are not really so. They may point to the frequent squabbles among women friends and shake their heads in disbelief. But who are they to speak for the women? Even Block and Greenberg do agree with Eichenbaum and Orbach. They say that "women also share a bond unique to them."

Block and Greenberg maintain that, "Unlike men, [women] are steeped in their physicality of menstruation, fertility, and birth ... Women share an awareness of their bodies that is uniquely female and, as such, is a link to one another." They believe that, "Perhaps it is women's ability to quickly understand and empathize with each other that makes them sought after as friends."[19]

I vividly recall the late evening in 1989 when my wife was about to give birth to our daughter and first child. I was not ready for the sudden outcry that the baby was forthcoming that day. We quickly began to call on friends who might assist in transporting us to Georgetown Hospital in Washington, D. C. The first person to promptly respond and arrive at our apartment was Mabel, a pastor's wife. Our male friends came after the baby was born.

The same thing happened one night in 1994 when our next child, a son was to be born. It was so sudden that we did not have the time to plan on who to call. The only person that my wife called that night was Maria, a friend of ours. She responded promptly. We were blessed to have someone who would care to respond to our need at past midnight.

Now, I am not ashamed to say that both helpers were our female friends. They understood what it was like to be under the pressure of delivering a baby -- even at night. No doubt, women empathize with each other much more and better than men. This is, of course, my subjective opinion.

The friendship story of Ruth and Naomi moves me to look forward with the hope that many women who read this chapter will respond to it with positive action. Such women must bring themselves to where they can become the Ruths and Naomis of our time. If this expectation is fulfilled, it would have been worthwhile to write this chapter and I will be immensely satisfied.

Figures indicate that there are more women than men on our planet, one reason being that women have a longer life expectancy than men. Wouldn't it be revolutionary if more and more women maintained real and abiding friendships? I personally believe that such a trend would be revolutionary. But such a movement must begin with you who has read this book. I am praying that you will begin one real friendship today. Someone around you is waiting for you to befriend him or her -- NOW.

# CHAPTER FIVE

# MAN-TO-MAN FRIENDSHIP

*Herein lies the tragedy of the age: not that men are poor...*
*But that men know so little of men.*

— W. E. B. DuBois, 1903

In the preceding chapter, we read that "women make the best friends." It would be misleading to assume that men are incapable of making the best friends. So, I must provide in this chapter an analysis of an excellent example of a male friendship which has become classic. This example is to be found in the Bible.

He is known to us as David, one of the most universally admired names in history. To the Moslems, he is known as Dawud. David ben Jesse (1018 - 978 B.C.) had one of the most loving and friendship relationships with Jonathan, the son of Saul Kish, king of ancient Israel.

C.S. Lewis placed this friendship at the same level with those of Pylades and Orestes, Roland and Oliver, and Amis and Amile. F.B. Meyer compared this friendship to that between Damon and Pythias in ancient or classical literature.[1]

Because most men know a lot about David and little about Jonathan, I shall provide a brief profile of Jonathan. In my view, he is really the hero of the friendship relationship which existed between the two men of Hebrew history.

## Jonathan's Profile

Jonathan's grandfather was a Benjamite, a wealthy elite man, "a mighty man of power" (I Sam. 9:1). His father, Saul, was appointed king by Samuel, and Saul became the political and military ruler of Israel from 1037 B.C. to 1018 B.C. Thus, Jonathan grew up in the royal palace as heir to the throne of Israel. Also, he was trained at the military academy. He commanded a troop of one thousand men.

With his father, Jonathan engaged in many military expeditions against Israel's hostile enemies, particularly, against the Philistines, their archenemy on the western frontier. Finis Jennings Dake tells us that there were twelve such expeditions during Saul's reign alone: seven against the Philistines, and one in each case against the Ammonites, the Moabites, the Edomites, the Syrians, and the Amalekites. It was a time for blood-letting and the town of Ephesdammin (which means "the boundary of blood") probably derived its name from those bloody wars.

There are indications in the biblical record that Jonathan had a successful career until the day he and his father and two other brothers perished in the battle against the Philistines at Mount Gilboa. Jonathan was a brave and courageous officer, a man with a daring and unflinching faith in the power of God to deliver his people from their enemies.

On one occasion, Jonathan and his bodyguard killed twenty Philistine soldiers during a surprising night raid. This military feat led to a spectacular victory for his father and for Israel. But it also led to trouble between him and his father who unreasonably had placed a curse upon his soldiers and starved them in the midst of a military operation.

Jonathan's perceptive mind had discerned that his father was misruling the people. After he had unknowingly violated his father's orders, he said: "My father hath troubled the land" (I Sam.14 : 29). This statement suggests that he did not approve of all of the policies of his father.

He believed that his father was pushing the soldiers to the extreme by disallowing the worn-out soldiers from tasting food, -- not even so much as a drop of honey! When his father ordered that Jonathan be executed, the soldiers rallied to his side and saved Jonathan's life.

It is evident that Jonathan was older than David, who later became his brother-in-law by marrying Michal, Jonathan's youngest sister. It is also very likely that Jonathan was present at the battle of Elah when David defeated and killed Goliath, the Philistine giant from Gath.

Something in their two personalities instantly drew them together into an indissoluble bond of friendship which generations of men and women have come to admire and respect. F.B. Meyer, in his book, *The Life of David: The Man After God's Own Heart*, summarizes the four distinctive qualities which Jonathan possessed and which made his friendship with David possible and strong. These qualities were:

### ◆ Maturity

Jonathan was as dexterous with the bow as his friend David was with the sling. He was strong, fearless and ready to defend this friend even at the cost of his own life. For this, his own father once threw the javelin at him! Elsewhere, I have written that a real man is one who is physically, spiritually, intellectually and financially mature. Jonathan was every inch a man. This is the kind of person who is often sought after for friendship.

### ◆ Sensitivity and Tenderness

Jonathan had the graces of strength, courage and endurance as well as a blending of the softer natures of sweetness and sympathy. He could weep with David and kiss him affectionately, soothing the sorrow-stricken and depressed future king during his most trying moments.

### ◆ Genuine Affection

Of this affection, the American author Finis Dake has said that "Jonathan made a covenant with David, because he loved him, and acknowledged that David would be the next king of Israel; he wanted some part in the kingdom under David." Unlike Saul, his father, Jonathan did not want to force God's hand in order to claim his birthright, the kingdom.

Because of this, Jonathan incurred the wrath of Saul, his father, when he spoke in David's favor. Saul not only insulted Jonathan publicly, but he actually tried to assassinate him. Dake points out that, "As a token of his great love for David and their covenant together, Jonathan stripped himself of his robe, his garments, and even his sword, bow and girdle."

"In the Middle East," Dake writes, "it was considered a special mark of respect to be presented, by a prince or sovereign, some piece of the garments he was wearing. The gift of a girdle was a special token of the greatest confidence and affection; and it was very highly prized ... Jonathan not only gave David one piece but the entire outfit he was wearing, including his weapons, which indicated that he was his servant altogether and owed complete allegiance to him."[2]

We should never at any time forget that, given our human propensity to selfishness and greediness, Jonathan could have manipulated David and collaborated with his father and sister to get rid of David. After all, David had been anointed king by the prophet Samuel and would therefore replace Jonathan as Israel's next monarch.

### ♦ Faith in God

We find this quality exhibited when Jonathan and his bodyguard raided the Philistine garrison and killed twenty soldiers.[3] At that moment, he had said: "There is no restraint to the Lord to save by many or by few" (1Sam. 14: 6). Such implicit faith and trust in God radiated a sense of self-confidence and self-assurance, qualities badly needed in any friendship.

Therefore, it is not surprising that we find that David was greatly shaken when news reached him that Jonathan had been killed at Mount Gilboa. On that sorrowful day, David exclaimed: "The beauty of Israel is slain upon thy high places: how are the mighty fallen!" (2 Sam. 1: 19). In this mournful lamentation, David revealed how deeply the marvelous love of Jonathan had affected him.

David referred to Jonathan as "my brother Jonathan: very pleasant hast thou been unto me: thy love to me was wonderful, passing the love of women" (2Sam. 1: 26). This was a very befitting eulogy for a dear friend. When some opportunists (expecting some reward) arrived to brag about how they had killed Jonathan, David promptly ordered one of his soldiers to take off their heads!

## David's Profile

David was Bethlehem's foremost minstrel and he came from a long line of historical figures: Ruth, Boaz, Obed, and Jesse who was the son of Obed. He was the youngest of eight children. His three brothers were already enlisted in Israel's army when Saul was king. While they worried with their king about the constant Philistine threat to their security, David wrestled with his father's wandering sheep in the wilderness.

The surprising attacks from a bear, or a lion, or whatever other creature nature allowed were sufficient for his attention. He was good at playing the harp and so good was he at it that when the royal court needed a musician to serve as a therapist for the frequently troubled king Saul, the national choice was David.

The Bible describes David as "rudy" but "of a beautiful countenance." He was charmingly handsome. In his romantic novel on the life of David, Frank Slaughter suggests that David's physical charm caught the eyes and heart of Michal, Saul's daughter.[4] Hence, we read: "And Michal ... loved David" (I Sam.18: 20). In the course of time, David married Michal, only to experience a marriage which was on a rocky, bumpy road from the very start.

David's shepherding years had prepared him well for the mature, brave and intelligent military ruler that he was to be. In those early years, with faith in God's power to deliver him from personal dangers, David single-handedly killed a bear and a lion that had attacked his father's sheep.

With such a faith, he also killed Goliath, a giant of a man from Philistia. The defeat of Goliath brought him national recognition and fame. He was described as "a mighty valiant man, and a man of war, and prudent in matters, and a comely person, and the LORD [was] with him" (I Sam. 16: 18).

Meanwhile, David was anointed and appointed king of Israel while Saul was still alive. Saul had disobeyed God and was to be replaced. David became the choice God had made. As he rose in fame and success, David fell out of Saul's favor. Saul became more and more jealous as the women sang David's praises for his great victory over Goliath. Also, Saul discovered that David would replace Jonathan on the throne. Thus, David became a fugitive in his own native land.

David continued to write his poems, compose his songs (known to us as the Psalms), and to sing his songs. He was not over-ambitious. He did not over-reach himself even though he knew he was king. He was quite a humble man, self-restrained and "a man after God's own heart" (I Sam. 13 :14). In time, David replaced Saul and ruled Israel from 1018 to 978 B.C.

### ◆ Surrender

He was not a typical autocrat. As we have noticed, his character is best illustrated by his merciful and forgiving spirit. He was not revengeful. Twice, he had the opportunity to kill Saul, his enemy, but he restrained himself for God's sake! After he became the king of Israel, he did not order the execution of Abner Ner, Saul's commander-in-chief. Centuries later, the ordinary people of Jerusalem referred to Israel's messiah as the "Son of David." No other person in Hebrew history has been given this kind of honor ever since.

## Their Bond of Friendship

Now, I would like to closely examine what cemented this friendship relationship between Jonathan and David. This bond of friendship emerged from the *blending* of their characters and the *fussion* of their areas of interests. The secret of this friendship was the unity of spirit and mission between the two men. "Can two walk together except they be agreed?" (Amos 3: 3)

In my judgment, this relationship between Jonathan and David was based upon the following fifteen characteristics:

### ◆ Spontaneity

It seems that theirs was an instant love -- love at first sight. The Scriptures tell us that "when [David] had made an end of speaking unto Saul, that the soul of Jonathan was knit with the soul of David, and Jonathan loved him as his own soul" (I Sam. 18: 1). This phrase, "loved him as his own soul," is repeated three times for our attention.

Following the great defeat of Goliath, David was summoned before king Saul. At the end of their discourse, for which Jonathan was present to observe this new unknown military hero, a spark of intense admiration and affection ignited within Jonathan.

He could not resist the temptation to love this new hero. The thrice-repeated statement reminds us that this was not to be a superficial outburst of emotion. It was rather so deep-rooted that Jonathan invited David to his pavilion that night. He embraced him and gave his most precious gifts to him.

### ♦ Covenant

The presentation of gifts was followed by the making of a covenant in which both men swore their faithfulness and commitment to each other. This was like a bridal festivity wherein each partner pledges to love and to cherish the other by oath. Again, we find that this covenant-making occurs three times (I Sam.18: 3; 20: 16; 23:18).

For many centuries, an agreement was sealed and ratified by swearing to an oath. One was not expected to break his oath. A man's oath was his bond. I recall that, not too long ago, some of my official documents, like the declaration of age, were sealed with an oath before the Justice of the Peace. If a person lied as he took the oath, he was in danger of perjurying himself. So it was for Jonathan and David. They had something legal and sacred to hold on to.

We read in I Samuel 18:4 that Jonathan stripped himself of the robe that was upon him, and gave it to David, along with his garments, sword, bow and girdle. I have already cited Dake's explanation of the implications of this action by Jonathan. What must also be realized is

that Jonathan's action also symbolized the inward stripping of his ego, pride and desire for the high office.
It was not long before David returned the same favor.

We notice that after Jonathan had discovered that his father Saul really intended to kill David, and helped David hide out in a field, "David arose out of a place toward the South, and fell on his face to the ground, and bowed himself three times...." (I Sam. 20:41). Obviously, the two men stripped themselves of their egocentricity and superiority complexes -- the two damning impediments to the growth of any true friendship.

### ♦ Fondness

"But Jonathan ... delighted much in David" (I Sam. 19: 2).
The intimation here is that of a man who is fond of his friend. We often speak of an absence which makes the heart grow fonder. The picture is that of a man who was pleasant to be with. Jonathan liked the presence of David because nothing irritated him.

The jovial, musical disposition of the Bethlehemite pleased Jonathan. Hence, he delighted in David who behaved himself wisely and well wherever he went.
David seemed to have the acceptance of all within the palace and outside of it. Who would not want such a person for a friend? Don't we often covet the company of someone who is held in high esteem and is the object of pride and admiration? Of course, we do, and so it was with Jonathan.

### ♦ Protection/Security

No friendship can survive for too long without this ingredient. Although he was the heir to the throne, and knew that he would someday be replaced by David, Jonathan still alerted David about the intentions of Saul to kill David. It was clear that Saul did not want David for a son-in-law.

Soon after David married Michal, news got to Jonathan of his father's plot and he promptly warned David: "My father Saul is looking for a chance to kill you. Be on your guard tomorrow morning, go into hiding and stay there. I will go out and stand with my father in the field where you are. I'll speak to him about you and will tell you what I find out" (I Sam.19: 2-3, NIV). Imagine being hunted by your father-in-law, the king, and being protected by your brother-in-law. What a circumstance!

Not once, but twice, Jonathan risked his own life to save David's. Every friendship needs this kind of ingredient because we all do occasionally find ourselves in hot water and in need of protection and safety from the many hazards of life. Nobody can claim that he is a good savior of himself or herself all of the time. We all do need someone else to care for us sometimes. Jonathan provided this kind of security for David. It was a wonderful paradox of intra-family feuds.

### ◆ Sound Advice

Along with the need for protection is the need for sound advice when we desperately need it from someone. I recall when I taught at Dillard University some years ago. I had left my Christian ministry in Nigeria to accept a late invitation to be employed at Dillard. After a few months, I found out that my job would be over. I was devastated.

A dear secretary at the Division of Social Sciences at the university saw through my deep hurts and provided me with some very good advice which I will never forget. Her sound advice has helped me cope with hurts ever since. So it was with David when he fled from the murderous palace of king Saul. Jonathan advised David to hide away while he sought out matters with his father, the king. Generally, when we feel surrounded and closed in by adversities, we rarely think straight. At such moments, we need a true friend's sound advice. It is refreshing to have such advice.

Eighteen years ago, when my dear mother passed away, I knew nothing about funeral arrangements. My father had always taken care of those kinds of things. This time, he seemed so distraught and disoriented that the responsibility fell upon me. Deaconess Ma Etuknwa of my home church at the time stepped in to provide her wise, loving care for all that was needed to be done. And, the funeral service was completed without much trouble to me. Jonathan did the same thing when David's prospects at the royal court turned dismal.

### ♦ Approval

No one needs a character assassinator for a friend. For any true friendship to survive, one must be willing to defend his friend's reputation when he or she is wrongly maligned. This is what Jonathan did for David when he spoke about him to his father, Saul.

Jonathan used good logic and wisdom to commend David. Jonathan reminded his father of the joy and gladness which David had brought to all on the day that he defeated Goliath. He argued that there was no evidence that David was plotting against Saul. Instead, he emphasized that David had constantly laid his life on the line in battles for the security of the nation.

Therefore, to kill David, he told Saul, was wrong. Such murder was tantamount to shedding innocent blood. There was no cause for the senseless crime. Saul listened and was persuaded. He seemed to have been momentarily convinced, at least. Saul reversed himself with an oath which he would soon break, for he was not a man of integrity.

### ♦ Restoration

Jonathan's approval of David had another practical effect. David was able to return to his former duties with less fear of danger. "He was in his presence, as in times past" (I Sam. 19: 7). In other words, David resumed his official duties, which included command of the troops, military expeditions, and playing the harp before the king when the king was troubled by an evil spirit (I Sam. 19: 9).

Like I said, Saul was not to be trusted. Once more, he tried one evening to assassinate David with his javelin. But David slipped away. Immediately, the king's murderers were hot upon the heels of David. This time, his wife, Michal alerted him and assisted him in his escape. Every friendship will need times of approval and restoration.

### ♦ Availability

We say that a friend in need is a friend indeed. Jonathan was truly a friend, indeed, for David. When he escaped from Saul, David sought refuge at Naioth, the home of the prophet Samuel who had anointed him to be king. He probably went there to find out why Samuel had brought all the problems upon him.

From Naioth, David came back looking for Jonathan.

He knew that Jonathan would be available for the kind of advice which he needed. Also, David probably wanted to relate to Jonathan what Samuel had said to him during his visit to Naioth. David was becoming a fugitive in his native land. So, he says to Jonathan: "What have I done? What is mine iniquity? And what is my sin before thy father, that he seeketh my life?" (ISam. 20: 1).

David continued: "If there be in me iniquity, slay me thyself; for why shouldest thou bring me to thy father?" (ISam. 20: 1, 8). Apparently, Jonathan was not aware that his father was still bent on killing David. David had to swear to Jonathan that this was so.

Since the new moon festival was about to begin and David had to be present at the palace, there was every possibility that Saul would seize this opportunity to kill David. David needed the mature advice of his friend. He had a scheme up his sleeves but needed to bounce it off Jonathan.

He would need to have an excuse for his absence during the festival and someone to relate it to the king. Who else was better suited as the harbinger of bad news to Saul than Jonathan? The two friends agreed that it was expedient that David hide away to test the honest intentions of the king (I Sam. 20:16).

### ♦ Assurance

When a dear friend is in trouble, sometimes he or she needs nothing more than the precious words of affirmation or assurance that all will be well. Even a criminal knows down deep within that he or she needs such assurances. There is something in all of us that craves for this assurance. This is what Jonathan offered to David before he was to be absent from the new moon festival.

It was Jonathan who assured David that he had a scheme to shoot some arrows in the direction of David's hide-out, to communicate if all was well or not at the palace. Sadly, it was not well at the palace for Jonathan himself. He had discovered that his father was still hell-bent upon murdering David. Saul had thrown the javelin at his own Jonathan after insulting him and his mother in very vulgar and abusive language.

Jonathan left the dinner table "in fierce anger" and shame. We have here a soberly-minded prince from a dysfunctional family who was trying to keep things together but with little success. But the two friends found solace and comfort, assurance and safety, in their faith in God. Each time they parted company from one another, they invoked the name of the Lord as the bedrock of their mutual friendship.

### ♦ Self-disclosure

Muriel James and Louis M. Savary stated that "self-disclosure is necessary in friendship."[5] They wrote that it is saying to a friend: "I feel so safe in your presence that I am willing to tell you things I wouldn't tell anyone else." They added: "Self-disclosure allows people to know themselves and to understand others."[6] Self-disclosure is a kind of taming one's friend.

Writing on the art of self-disclosure, Alan Loy McGinnis said that "People with deep and lasting friendships may be introverts, extroverts, young, old, dull, intelligent, homely, good-looking; but the one characteristic they always have in common is openness. They have a certain transparency, allowing people to see what is in their hearts."[7]

McGinnis considered this transparency the second

most important rule for deepening any friendship.

According to him, Betty Ford, the wife of one of America's former presidents, possessed this kind of transparency. We find the same kind of transparency in the Jonathan-David friendship. They were maskless.

When David shared with Jonathan his scheme to run away to Bethlehem, his hometown, for the yearly family sacrifice, this was an act of self-disclosure. In all probability, there was no such yearly family sacrifice. It was merely a scheme, an excuse, to escape from Saul. Jonathan understood this "white lie" and collaborated with it without betraying his friend. The scheme gave Jonathan the chance to test his father's murderous intentions. And, David was proved right.

During the discourse which followed the unveiling of this scheme, Jonathan made his own self-disclosure -- his fear about the future of his family (I Sam. 20: 9,15). He told David that he was fully aware that he would be the next king. But, he wanted David to swear to him that his descendants would be protected by David.

We do not find any trace of anger or even jealousy on the part of Jonathan regarding this matter. Instead, Jonathan succeeds in obtaining a solemn promise, an oath from David, that he would show kindness to Jonathan's family when David became the next king of Israel. Jonathan's honesty in this matter is superbly transparent. His behavior is almost beyond human comprehension, for heirs to the throne do not lightly give up their inheritance.

### ◆ Prayer of a Beloved

Somewhere, I have hinted at this ingredient. But, it is worth repeating. There was a spiritual dimension in the

Jonathan-David relationship. We find glimpses of this throughout the biblical narrative. In the first book of Samuel 20: 12-14, the term LORD is used four times. There, Jonathan seems to intercede for David. Jonathan's declaration to help is also a prayer: "And Jonathan said unto David, O LORD God of Israel ..."

Prayer will always enrich a friendship, whether it be between spouses in the home, or between friends at work, at school, in the prisons, in the air as one flies, or in the bottom of the sea if one finds himself in a submarine. Prayer is the one thing that our enemies can do nothing about. Something is lost when a relationship is without it. Prayer is the soul's sincere desire, uttered or unexpressed. Our true friends should always be able to count upon our prayers.

### ♦ "The Message of the Arrows"

When we read I Samuel 20: 25-40, we find another important action of Jonathan which powerfully communicated his love and friendship for David. Author F.B. Meyer has termed this action "the message of the arrows."[8] Love has its own unique language and messages.

For instance, I have a precious friend who still lives in the village where I grew up and, between us, we have a nickname known only to both of us. Recently, I received a letter from this friend. He addressed me by my nickname. As I read it, a warm smile brushed over my face. We have known each other by these nicknames for over thirty years.

Even so, Jonathan used the shooting of some arrows to communicate to his friend, David, whether or not there was any danger awaiting him at the royal palace. I believe that every relationship ought to have its own vocabulary. This is what makes such a relationship unique. As Meyer has shown, such a vocabulary communicates a unique message to a special friend when it is needed.

Meyer wrote that "the arrows taught that a strong and noble friend was standing in the breach." Not even Saul himself could have detected that David was not at Bethlehem, but behind a rock in the field. The lad sent to pick up the arrows did not know what was happening. David's "secret place" was known only to Jonathan and to God.

Later, David would refer to it as "the secret place of the most High" (Psalm 91:1). Jonathan was not ashamed to own up to his friendship with David, even though doing so annoyed and frustrated his father. Also, he was not ashamed to speak up for the cause of truth.

Meyer states that the arrows warned David of imminent danger. David had to go away from the company of his beloved friend. Had he lingered around the palace, David's life would have been lost. The arrows taught that it was time to separate from Saul and his family. Their love had to suffer from this separation.

In many cases, our human love and friendships will suffer from times of separation. This separation may come by death or by relocation. Nevertheless, we must learn to bear with our friends. Our love will abide and continue because it is concrete and real.

### ◆ Humility

Throughout this discussion, we do not find any trace of pomposity, arrogance or vain pride between Jonathan and David. I Sam. 20:41, describes a true picture of humility: "And as soon as the lad was gone, David arose out of a place toward the South, and fell on his face to the ground, and bowed himself three times: and they kissed one another, and wept one with another, until David exceeded." In other words, David emerged from his hideout and wept uncontrollably for a long time.

It takes real humility for a man to weep. It takes even a greater degree of humility for two brave military officers to show their tears in public. Soldiers are generally drilled in a manner that would result in boldness and bravery, not weakness. This was not entirely true of Jonathan and David. Their boldness was subdued by their humility to weep.

### ♦ Kisses and Tears of Love

Some people find it difficult to kiss in public. I do. I think mainly because of my cultural background. However, every friendship ought to have its way of expression of the feelings. It could be a warm embrace, a loving look, a warm smile, a twinkling of an eye, a firm grip of the hand and so forth. But, for Jonathan and David, it was the kissing and shedding tears of love.

We do not know if they kissed each other on the lips or on the cheeks. Whatever mode it was, the kissing spoke of true love from the heart. Moreover, their kissing was mingled with the tears of sorrow and comfort for each other. David was about to separate from Jonathan.

Both men knew that this was necessary. What they did not know was when they would meet again. Jonathan could only say to David: "Go in peace," and he also reminded him once more of their oath "in the name of the LORD." The two wonderful friends never met again after this incident until Saul was out in pursuit of David again, to kill him.

The Keilites had betrayed David by informing Saul that David was hiding out in a mountain in the wilderness of Ziph. Jonathan accompanied his father during this trip. As the Bible text shows, he was not a part of the murderous party. He was not there to apprehend David. Rather, "Jonathan Saul's son arose, and went to David into the wood, and strengthened his hand in God" (I Sam. 23 :16).

It is not entirely clear whose hand was strengthened. Whichever it was, Saul went out to commit murder, but Jonathan went out for mutual spiritual reunion and refreshment with his friend. Sadly, this was their last meeting. Soon afterwards, both Saul and Jonathan died in the battle of Mount Gilboa.

I have taken pains to highlight these fifteen ingredients in the Jonathan-David friendship because I believe that many so-called friendships today lack many of these elements. There seems to be few genuine friendships especially among men these days. Dr. Susan Jeffers cites a 1983 study of two hundred men and women in which two-thirds of the men in that group could not name a best friend. Of those who could, the best friend was likely to be a woman.[9]

I'd like to encourage men reading this that it is not impossible to initiate and develop the Jonathan-David kind of genuine friendship. What I believe is difficult is the readiness and willingness to pay the price for this kind of relationship. Dr. Jeffers points out one of the common problems associated with men in building friendships that they should be aware of.

She writes that "Men won't open up because they have been taught that in order to survive in the society in which they have been raised, you keep your feelings to yourself. Very little has changed over the years. Men will stay that way until it's safe to let it all out.... openness is still equated by too many with weakness, homosexuality, dependency, and other characteristics thought of as unmanly."[10]

The impact of this negative belief about men formed over many years has been devastating. Many women, therefore, she claims believe that "Men give you pain. Men fear commitment. Men lie. Men fool around. Men are inconsiderate."[11] But, we ought to notice that these five statements are mere generalizations. They form part of the male-bashing and the "waiting-to-exhale" syndrome or mentality which is held by many women.

Jeffers provides in her book a list of what she calls some "appreciating affirmations" about men that "ought to be repeated at least once a day with gusto!"[12] These affirmations include the fact that men are sweet; men are kind; men are wonderful; men can be truthful; men can and do commit; men can be reliable.

Dr. James W. Pennebaker, in his book *Opening Up*, flatly states that opening up provides a healing power. In another work, what the *Boston Globe* called "a probing study," Stuart Miller also speaks to men who yearn for more meaningful contacts with other men. Miller contends that genuine friendships are possible between men.[13]

We must realize that Jonathan and David were not "just friends" in the Lillian Rubin sense but *real friends*, in actuality, as Caroline J. Simon, a Philosophy Professor at Hope College, Holland, Michigan, showed in an essay on friendship.[14] As we come to the end of this chapter, I would like to reiterate some of the important points which made the Jonathan-David friendship feasible:

1. This friendship was one which cut across

generational and class lines. Jonathan was older than David and much more experienced in military and political matters. David was from the ordinary group of shepherd men. Jonathan was of the monarchical, elite class. David was rustic, a lad from the agricultural class.

Both men probably or certainly knew of their differences, however, they did not matter to them. Their differences were covered by real love. A marvelous bond of friendship brought and held them together. Their love for each other cut away selfishness, greediness, political manipulation and the ambitions which would have destroyed their friendship.

2.  This friendship was grounded upon the willingness to depend on each other mutually. There was nothing of the rugged individualism common in our time. Dr. Marion F. Solomon writes about this willingness to depend upon our friends and calls it "the power of positive dependency."

Marion Solomon argues that, after thirty years of experience in helping couples, the single most important lesson for strengthening relationships is to abandon the misconception that dependency signifies a childlike neediness and that self-sufficiency is the hallmark of psychological health. "No man or woman is an island,"[15] she insists. She brands this notion of self-sufficiency a myth.

3.  This friendship survived because the wives of Jonathan and David did not obstruct the relationship. The two friends were militarily and politically engaged but their wives did not intrude foolishly into their matters. In fact, once, Michal, David's wife, assisted in the

enhancement of the success of this friendship by abetting the plans of David to escape from her father. Men need space for the growth of male friendships.

Also, both men were honest in their relationship toward their wives. We do not read of any of the playboy or Hollywood kinds of infidelity and fornication. No one was sleeping with his or her friend's husband, wife, sister, or daughter and later made sport (a movie) out of it for public consumption.

4. This friendship was not based upon "free sex" and the hedonism that is so common today. It was not built upon a search for the gratification of every carnal desire. So, we find no elements of lesbianism, cross-sexual, or homosexual practices between Jonathan and David.

Stuart Miller stated that in America and in Europe he encountered the notion that "the fear of being taken for a homosexual or, worse, becoming one [was] a main factor keeping adult men from close friendships."[16] He commented that the universality of this notion was astonishing. He argued that this notion was not the decisive factor in restraining male friendships. There are other factors, such as economic and social.

Miller cited C.S. Lewis' book, *The Four Loves*, (which I analyzed in Chapter Two), and explained that the equation of male friendship with homosexuality was not a new problem. Lewis had examined this matter. So also had Edward Garnett in his 1927 study of the problem. Both Garnett and Lewis had made strong arguments that male friendships could exist and flourish which did not include homosexuality.

Miller concluded that, in fact and in practice, there is a difference between male friendship and homosexuality. Only the most deranged individual would equate the two matters. He noted that this matter seemed to be a Western problem. He noticed that in Asia and Africa, there was no fear of male friendship resorting to homosexuality.

In Asia and Africa, men and women may "sleep" with each other without sexual intercourse. They can hold hands and kiss in public without any embarrassment.[17] In our day, when homosexuality and lesbianism are on the up-swing, should we not return to the Jonathan-David kind of friendship, to platonic love?

5. The Jonathan-David friendship was rooted in faith in a higher being -- God. Modern friendship, lacking a godly component -- that is, a reverence and consideration of the spiritual -- is bound to be shallow, dishonorable, and insincere. With these characteristics come all the manipulative and destructive tendencies inherent in modern friendship relations. If we are to have good friendships, we must include the element of the spiritual for such friendships to transcend mere carnality.

I love the words of Edwin L. Cole when he writes: "l like men. I like a man's man. I like men of worth, value, character. I like real men. I don't like the pussyfooting pipsqueaks who tippy toe through the tulips. I like men to be men."[19] And, a little gray-haired lady in his listening audience thundered back, "Amen!" in response.

I believe that Jonathan and David would have similarly responded to Dr. Cole. I pray that you, too, will respond by initiating one real friendship today.

# CHAPTER SIX

# FRIENDSHIP IN THE HOME

*There's no place like home.*
--- John Howard Payne, 1791-1852

Sir Edward Coke (1552 - 1634) is credited with the statement that "one's home is the safest refuge to everyone." Irving Berlin, who wrote the song "God Bless America" in 1938, considered the United States of America "home sweet home!" Home is where any family resides. And happy is the home where friendship dwells.

A family without friendship among its members is like a tree without a sap -- lifeless. It's a matter of time before the wind of disaster tears such a tree apart. Much has been said of late about home and the family. But very little and almost nothing has been written about friendship within the family.

My task in this chapter is to examine this kind of relationship -- the friendship between a husband and his wife, friendship between parents and their children, friendship among the children themselves and friendship which includes the extended members of a family, such as cousins, nieces, nephews, uncles, aunts, grandparents, grandchildren and in-laws.

During the George Bush presidency, former Vice President Dan Quayle made the headlines when he decried the condition of the American family. This condition is about the fact that although there are 68.8 million families in the United States and 33.9 million contain children under the age of eighteen, more and more households are *not* families.[1]

Today, the number of women living alone in America is 14.2 million and the number of men living alone is 9.4 million. The number of unmarried couples living together is about 3.5 million.[2] It is estimated that there are 1.6 million cohabiting gay and lesbian couples in the United States, and about 2 million gay parents.[3]

Seventy-percent of all black babies currently being born are born to single mothers out of wedlock.[4] Almost one-third of all American children (and two-thirds of African-American children) are now born out of wedlock. Up to sixty-five percent of all new marriages now fail.[5] This is the sorry condition of the family in America.

In his recent book, *The American Family*, Dan Quayle suggests that the family is made up of a father, a mother, and the children. He seems to ignore the current popular acceptance of the single-parent "family." He does not define what a family is, neither does he include friendship in his list of the ten things which can make American families strong.[6] His book highlights five examples of the ideal, successful family across America, from the state of Maine in the northeast to Hawaii in the Pacific coast.

Since Quayle has not succinctly told us what the family is, we need to consider other views. Thomas Moore, who is widely known for his book, *Care of the Soul*, and for his psychological and philosophical insights, writes that "a family is not an abstract cultural ideal: a man, a woman, and children living blissfully in a mortgaged house on a quiet neighborhood street."

Rather, he continues, "the family the soul wants is a felt network of relationship, an evocation of a certain kind of interconnection that grounds, roots, and nestles.... The soul family is an echo, a poetic reverberation of the literal family; it exists in the time of myth even before an actual family gives it life."[7] Definitely, Moore departs from the concrete impressions of Quayle and takes us to the higher realms of the spiritualization of the idea of the family.

Amy E. Dean walks the same path as Moore in her exposition on "family soul" and the home. She writes that "the home ... is not so much a place in which there is material or physical comfort but a space that provides emotional and spiritual comfort -- a place that does not change even when the person, or world around the person, changes."[8]

Dean insists that "what fosters a family spirit more is not an actual living space or its contents, but the space in which each family member can merge heart and mind, and fashion his or her soul by rooting it in a personally soul-stimulating retreat."[9]

Frankly, many a family member is not concerned

about the soulishness or the spiritualization of the family in the sense in which Thomas Moore or Amy Dean has provided. Most  family members are mainly concerned with the tangible aspects of everyday life. Hence, we still need another practical definition of the family or home.

I prefer the definition which Ruth Westheimer offers. Popularly known as Dr. Ruth, a psychosexual therapist residing in New York, Westheimer writes that "A family is a group of people linked together by some combination of love, commitment, cohabitation, children, bloodlines, memories, and thoughts about the future."[10]

She adds: "It's a matter of connection -- with each other, with a shared past and future, and with generations before and since. And it's a matter of responsibility. When you're in a family, you don't need to see each other every day, or even every week, but you need to know, unconditionally, that if necessary, those people will be available to you."[11] This is a very useful definition.  Her definition is comprehensive and contains some of the ingredients of friendship which we analyzed in Chapter Two.

In addition to those of Quayle, Moore, Dean, and Dr. Ruth, there are other voices which have spoken in support of strengthening the American family and home. David Blankenhorn seems to have set the alarm bell ringing with his *Fatherless America* in 1995. He was joined by the American First Lady Hillary Clinton, with her *It Takes A Village* (1995).  The previous year, the former Secretary of Education under the Reagan presidency, William J. Bennett, had sounded a warning with the book, *The De-Valuing of Family.*[12]

To the best of my knowledge, none of these voices has embraced the notion that familial friendship is important. My position, therefore, is that many families are breaking up and collapsing today because its members have abandoned the concept of family friendship or have refused to work in the commandment of love.

For various reasons beyond the scope of this book, family members have practically become hostile and enemies to each other. It's past time to rediscover the importance of being friends within the family.

## Husband and Wife Friendship

Dr. Joel D. Block and Diane Greenberg posed the question, " is there friendship after marriage?" in chapter six of their book *Women & Friendship*. My answer is definitely "yes." Block and Greenberg positively agreed. A man and his wife ought to be friends before and after they are married. And why not?

Does it make any sense that couples who before they were married and found themselves in sweet romantic love should thereafter become sworn enemies and hostile to each other? If so, then many people are better advised to refrain from marriage. Why hurt yourself if your spouse is ever to remain your enemy after marriage? This is simply not what most decent and sensible people want.

Block and Greenberg discovered that the maintenance of family friendship between a husband and his wife is a surprisingly difficult task. Ideally, married partners are *supposed* to be best friends. But, in practice and historically, this has not been the case. Unfortunately, most husbands and wives often fight like cats and dogs.

In pre-industrial societies, including America, women were not expected to have friendships outside the family. Marriage was intended solely for the purposes of procreation, sexual satisfaction, and economics. The woman's emotional needs, feelings, and interests were not taken seriously. Her world revolved around that of her husband and children. As a result, honest and true intimacy between the sexes was nearly non-existent.

Even where there is a semblance of family friendship, this usually occurs among the couples. It is known as "couple-to-couple friendship." The notion of couple-to-couple friendship, Block and Greenberg noted, is relatively recent, and emerged from about the 1930's in the United States. Couple friendships have their setbacks, e.g., lack of privacy, trust, and total communion needed for true intimacy.

Also, in this type of group or couple friendship, there is often the possibility of jealousies, particularly, where one member of a family becomes too fond of or is attracted to a member of the opposite sex in the other family.[13] Also, another drawback of this kind of friendship is that very few couples would allow their partners to maintain an individual and separate friendship outside of the marriage.

The reasons for this attitude are many, including personal insecurities, immaturity, and suspicion of abandonment or even the fear that a partner may wind up in bed with another person of the opposite sex. The pressures from these kinds of attitudes add to the loss of trust and intimacy. There is also the problem of time for closeness between husband and wife, especially when children are involved.

During the early years of child-rearing, there's usually very little time for intimacy. In my own experience, I find that lovemaking occurs frequently at night after the children have gone to bed and are deep asleep. Sometimes, my wife and I are so tired that sex is impossible and has to be postponed. Our children's needs have taken priority over our own needs. There is need for us to be patient and tolerant.

Many husbands and their wives react to the lack of time for each other and to the pressures of raising their children by living in separate emotional worlds. They do this out of selfishness. Perhaps, they had come from families where friendship was never important. Instead of working out their own friendships, they give in to complaining which is rooted in selfishness.

According to Eichenbaum and Orbach, "A woman comes to marriage expecting and yearning for a partner who will understand her deeply, accept her, and be there for her to lean on emotionally, but all too often she finds that her partner is frightened of intimacy, steers away from emotional contact and discussion, and is somewhat frightened or put off by her needs."

They add: "Whereas, in some sense, her husband continues to receive mothering, she does not. Therefore her unconscious expectations, desire for both a nourishing connection as well as a supported autonomy, is rarely achieved."[14] I believe that, in general, many such women feel that marriage is a necessary evil.

Some psychology experts say that instead of offering women the expected protection, emotional fulfillment, friendship and a bolstered identity, marriage brings to many women subjugation, the draining of their emotions, servitude and the blurring of their self-image. Women feel that most men are less empathic to their emotional needs than they are to their husband's.

"Empathy is the ability to imagine or think about another person's condition .... Empathy is a conscious process whereby one attempts to understand the experience of another."[15] Hence, many women are frustrated in their marriages and, more than men, retain separate friendships among themselves after marriage.

Block and Greenberg explained that many people often confuse infatuation with real love. With increasing deception, there is bound to be no basis for intimacy. Some women even believe that the average man tells a--thousand-and-one lies to women. When these kinds of "lovers" do marry, their premarital friendship soon fizzles out or changes.

Therefore, Block and Greenberg admonished that, for those persons intending to marry, it is best to consider what friendship means to them *before* marriage. Also, these kinds of people should consider how their own friends will influence their lives after marriage. In reality, these matters are rarely seriously considered or discussed. The passion for romance and "falling in love" usually take precedence. "A large part of the daily emotional nourishment," Block and Greenberg wrote, "springs not from romance but from friendship."[16]

According to Block and Greenberg, one important enhancer of friendship between a husband and his wife is meaningful communication. This is not the communication about such superficialities as the weather, the children's report cards, the rising cost of food, and the hardship of doing laundry. There's no fun in these kinds of communication.

Block and Greenberg maintained that, "Openness of communication is an excellent source of marital friendship."[17] It's pretty common knowledge that a marriage will succeed in proportion to the degree of intimacy between a husband and his wife. But, again, bearing in mind the current divorce rate, "friendship in marriage is a goal accomplished by too few."[18] This means that probably only a small percentage of married couples engage in meaningful communication which could lead to family friendships.

Also, Block and Greenberg disclosed that people who are less possessive of their spouses are more likely to succeed in family friendship. They found that women who work, who had been to college, who have independent, stimulating, have outside interests like hobbies and games, more often consider their husbands to be friends. [19]

Dr. Claire Rabin, who is a social worker and therapist at the Bob Shappell School of Social Work at Tel Aviv University in Israel, sees the solution to the problems associated with family friendship differently. Having examined the connection between inequality in marriage and marital distress, Rabin stresses the key role of friendship in establishing a truly equal relationship. She believes that friendship is "the basic condition of equal partnership"[20] between a husband and his wife.

Block and Greenberg observed that "it is difficult to imagine how revolutionary the idea is that wives and husbands should be friends with each other."[21] And truly, as I said in my analysis of woman-to-woman friendships, I agree with Block and Greenberg that the idea of real friendship between a husband and his wife is revolutionary indeed.

For me, the central issue is that a husband be fair and considerate toward his wife, as the Bible teaches. This is the basis of my friendship with my wife. Fairness and consideration interprets into washing the dishes as often as possible (especially if she did the cooking), cooking for the family when she is out working and I am at home, changing the diapers, putting the children to bed on time at night, helping to keep the house tidy, and inviting her to watch a particular television program with me which I consider mutually important or interesting.

Fairness and consideration also mean that I minimize

complaining about everything, but instead show the example of leadership in the home. A husband must be the C.E.O in the home and lead well. It also means that I be sensitive to her anxieties, like in a recent case when she received a midnight call and discovered that her mother was gravely ill.

I believe that if there is a good amount of fair treatment, consideration, praying together and talking together, the basis of friendship would thus be established and maintained. Aren't these the things that couples do? In my family situation, our friendship is centered around our common faith in Jesus Christ who is the head of our home. And we both like it that way.

## Child-Parent Friendship

"Friendship in childhood is not a mere luxury; for optimal functioning it is an imperative."[22] For a child's social development, early friendship with the parents is supremely important.

You probably have heard of the "toxic parents" and of the "narcissistic father." The idea of toxic parents was popularized by Dr. Susan Forward in 1989 by her book of that name. She gave the following six characteristics of the toxic parent:

- ♦ inadequate parents
- ♦ alcoholics
- ♦ verbal abusers
- ♦ physical abusers
- ♦ sexual abusers, and
- ♦ controllers.

Toxic parents are the kind of parents who tell their child(ren) that they are bad and worthless. They use physical pain in discipline. They demand that their children take care of *them* because of their own problems. They are couples who use fear and intimidation to secure compliance, obedience, and respect from their children. They are the kind of parents who commit incest and other forms of sexual abuses against their children.[23]

Such parents can hardly experience true friendship between themselves and their children. Their children have been deprived of early empathic care. As John Leopold Weil has ably shown, such deprivations have grave consequences upon the proper growth and development of a child.[24] How many parents today are suffering from the loss of friendship from their adult children because they had been toxic parents?

In the case of the narcissistic couple, "the narcissistic dad requires that his children (particularly his sons) excel and stand out so that he can vicariously experience the son's excellence as his own. Conversely, the son's struggles and failures also become the father's own, so that he rejects the child in order to distance himself from sharing in failure."[25]

Dr. Joan Lachkar writes that "narcissists are individuals who need perfect mirroring, perfect stroking, perfect responses. Narcissists need to be in control. When injured or insulted, they typically withdraw or isolate themselves." Narcissism is a kind of marital pathology. Lachkar has this fuller description:

"Narcissists are driven by the need to be desired and appreciated, tend to isolate themselves either physically or emotionally, fear a loss of specialness, and are easily injured or outraged when not properly understood. They are dominated by guilt and self-hatred, and have idealized and omnipotent fantasies."

She adds: "Preoccupied with a loss of self-regard, narcissists have an over-investment in self, yet will do anything to preserve a sense of specialness, and attempt to prove themselves by isolation from others and concentration on perfection, power, and omnipotence."[26] Truly, many of us have met these kinds of people sometime and somewhere in our lives.

In the world of the narcissists, the common thread is skewed responsibility. Stephanie Donaldson-Pressman and Robert M. Pressman say that the narcissistic family is one in which "the needs of the parent system took precedence over the needs of the children .... The responsibility of needs fulfillment shifts from the parent to the child."[27]

Personally, I believe that toxic parenting and narcissistic fathering are two of the most significant obstacles to the friendship between children and their parents. Block and Greenberg say that "there is no question among authorities on child development that friendless children are more susceptible to emotional disturbances. Childhood friends are our first link with the world outside our family."[28]

Heather Smith concurs with Block and Greenberg when she asserts that when children's emotional needs are not met, they become unhappy. "Unhappy children reveal their distress both at home and at school through fear, anxiety and often troublesome [behaviour] which is not easy to comprehend or to handle."[29]

As the head of our family, my aim is not to be a toxic or narcissistic father, but to maintain the friendship relationship with my wife, my daughter and my son. The greatest gifts which a father can offer to his home are love and availability. I also agree with Rollo May that "the basic relationship between a father and son is the essence of healthy living."[30]

At a time when fathering is in short supply and permissiveness is widespread, youngsters are often unruly, rebellious, and irresponsible.[31] A man therefore has to be available to his family and provide the necessary love. I strive to be such a father without pretending to be perfect or a know-it-all dad.

Victoria Secunda points out that there are six different kinds of fathers: the doting, distant, demanding, seductive, absent, and good-enough father. I want to be the sixth kind in her list, especially since, according to her, "All fathers are, at first, heroes to their daughters."[32] She also maintains that a mother and her daughter can be (yes!) friends.[33]

And let me be very clear here. My spouse and I do not believe that providing friendship for our children means giving them license to do whatever they please. That is not a biblical standard or prescription. We mean, in the words of Dr. James Dobson, the guru on family relations, "tough love" for our children. We mean, in the sense of Rodney S. Patterson, friendship which provides "a sense of support, emotional exchange, assistance, and fun."[34]

In my home, the friendship with our children involves my playing "moo-oo" with them. I get on all fours, my son or my daughter (and sometimes both of them) then climb onto my back and ride me like a rodeo or horse or cow while I shout "moo-oo." Sometimes, I take my daughter out for an evening walk, pointing her to the beauty of the flowers, the moon, and stars. We also eat out as a family. These activities are intended to provide quality time for conversation without the many distractions often present in the home.

I also read bed-time stories to my children and sing

them to sleep sometimes to help strenthen the relationship. We also go to church together as a family where I teach Sunday School and my daughter participates in missionettes' meetings. My spouse seeks out cultural programs such as the Red Cross and summer soccer camps for our daughter. We watch them play with the neighborhood children and try to ensure that their lives are full of fun.

We also teach our children principles relating to morals, values and individual responsibility. We insist on discipline and respect for authority. As parents, we believe that it is not the state or country's business to intrude into how we raise our children. We believe in laying down our lives for our children, bearing in mind what our Savior said: "Greater love had no man than this, that a man laid down his life for his friends" (John 15:13). In short, we believe in "spiritual parenting" as Hugh and Gayle Prather have maintained.[35]

## Friendship Among Children

Generally speaking, children are friendly to each other until adults corrupt them. Children are greatly influenced by their environment. Watching my children grow up in the United States has confirmed in my heart that all the racial theories regarding black inferiority are baseless. No child was ever born a racist or ethnicist.

Children are naturally very tender-hearted, quick to forgive and forget. They respond to one another readily. I have drawn these observations from watching children play. Jesus of Nazareth said that a person cannot enter into the kingdom of God unless he or she received it like a child (Lk. 18: 17). Thus, the Savior had a high view of children

I am not impressed by the many books on sibling rivalry written by adults, many of who are fathers that have been poor at child-rearing. Many fathers are failures in parenting and the evidence of this is overwhelming. In the United States, the media has compounded matters by the useless things shown on television. Sadly, thousands of innocent children are abused and abandoned daily.

Mary Pipher, who has examined why more American adolescent girls are prey to depression, eating disorders, addictions and suicide attempts than ever before, writes that "we live in a look-obsessed, media-saturated, 'girl-poisoning' culture."[36] Add to this poisoning, the incredible number of cases of incest and child-prostitution. Why should we wonder why the children in America are so rebellious and unfriendly to the adults around them? We have become a culture that exploits and brutalizes children!

William J. Bennett reminds us that the friends which our children keep are very important. He writes: "Every parent knows how crucial the choice of friends is for every child. Childhood friendships tell parents which ways their children are tending. They are important because good friends bring you up, and bad friends bring you down. So it matters who our children's friends are. And it matters, as examples to our children, who our friends are .... We must teach children how to recognize counterfeit friends, to know they are injurious, to realize they reinforce what is less than noble in us."[37]

What Bennett is pointing to is the need to provide our children with the tools which encourage and promote sibling and teenage friendships. In this regard, Susan Alexander Yates, a mother of five who resides in Falls Church, Virginia, has marvelously offered such tools through her book, *A House Full of Friends: How To Like the Ones You Love* (1995).

She analyzes family friendships in all its dimensions, including friendship in the early, middle, and later years of adolescence. She affirms that "it is still possible to cultivate a family marked by friendship ... We can still grow in friendship and love as a family ... You can still become a family of friends."[38]

I believe that if parents would teach their children to be godly, reverent and obedient to God's laws through their love for Him, and if parents would show children that God really loves them, it is possible for such children to know God as their friend and thus project and communicate this friendship to people around them. They need to know that our God is loving and friendly.

I do not imply that children cannot use their willpower to disobey or even hate God. Much of what children see today in the name of religion turns them off. For many children, their parents' God is a drug, without any joyful experience that comes from the transforming power of Jesus Christ. But God's grace is still sufficient to induce the spirit of friendship from our children. The community would profit as societal crimes, particularly, juvenile-related crimes, diminish because of the impact of friendly and godly homes upon the children.

## Extended Family Friendship

Since family friendship is possible, there is no reason why it should not include members of one's extended family. Every family has its extended branches -- grandparents, uncles, aunts, cousins, nephews, nieces, grandchildren, and the in-laws. The extended family system is very important and prominent in African culture.

Derek S. Hopson and Darlene Powell Hopson,

practicing clinical psychologists, write that "the legacy of the extended family, which had its origins in Africa, is still thriving in the homes of many African Americans." They point out that it is not unusual to find that many children in the black community have been raised by their grandparents, aunts, uncles and other kin. "If an extended family is central to your life," they say, "you are a part of something very special but you probably also experience its complications."[39]

Believing that "the traditional family isn't working,"[40] Karen Lindsey strongly argues that families can be created anywhere and that friends can become one's own family. The implication is that a narrow definition of family as incorporating only a man, woman, a child or children and a pet, is no longer tenable. In her book, *Friends As Family* (1981), Lindsey shows that the extended family is important and that the word family must embrace a broader definition.

Again, Susan Alexander Yates provides valuable insights as to how to broaden our friendship to include the members of our extended family. She offers six ways to do this: maintenance of a positive attitude, learning from them, phoning, visiting, and celebrating with them, caring for them, having a sense of humor when they are around, and preparing "to look back with a sense of gratitude rather than a feeling of regret"[41] when any of them dies.

Although these six things are directed primarily toward the in-laws, they can apply to our extended family members as a whole. Yates also lists some forty-one things which grandparents can do with their grandchildren.[42] Chapter fifteen of her book is devoted to caring for the extended family.

When I first began to think about this topic on

familial friendships, I observed that very little or nothing has been written on this subject. Indeed, Susan Alexander Yates' book is the only comprehensive work that I know of at the moment. I still believe that more work should be done to encourage friendships in the home.

Beyond the philosophizing and articulation about friendship in the home, a lot depends upon the practice of what we believe and preach. Everyone belongs to some kind of family or home. We must therefore seriously consider how a new attitude of friendship can revolutionize and enrich our lives, our societies and our world. My earnest prayer is that your home and family will begin to become a family of love and of friends.

# CHAPTER SEVEN

# FRIENDSHIP AT
# THE WORKPLACE

*There is nothing more fatal to friendship than the greed of gain.*

--- Cicero

It is likely that your instinctive reaction to this chapter's title is surprise or even shock. You may be saying to yourself: "Friendships At Work? My boss is silly over business (S. O. B). He or she does not (and never would) let me get ahead."

You may vividly recall the last time you were denied a promotion and as a result you burned with anger or rage. Or, you may have constantly been by-passed for a raise or promotion because of your boss or supervisor. You're probably right -- your boss is an S.O.B. Indeed, there may be many of them still around these days.

The good news is that there are also many wonderful people at your workplace with whom genuine friendship is still possible. These are the Sons of God (S. O. G.), the people of God. They are usually the more caring, empathic and morally conscious co-workers you need. But, you've got to discover them.

## Conventional Workplace Environment

You should not be surprised I said that there may be many S. O. G.'s around. Dr. Joel D. Block and Diane Greenberg said: "The structure of the business world is derived from the military, while its everyday functioning is governed by the rules of team sports."[1]

If you have ever had the slightest acquaintance with that impressive institution, you would find out that the first order in the military is obedience to commands -- not logic, reason, or intimacy. A soldier quickly learns that authority is the military's first law of survival. Authoritarianism is the key philosophical basis for the smooth running of the military.

So, when Block and Greenberg tell us that the structure of the business world is derived from the military, we should understand what they mean. They imply that the business world includes men and women whose only idea of how to run things is to be bossy. And I mean really bossy and authoritarian. Unfortunately, these are the kinds of bosses who have no room for friendships at the workplace.

The conventional wisdom of these kinds of people at the top is for them to look out just for number one in order to catch up with the Jones'. For them, the dollar is the bottom line. These kinds of bosses never think of feelings, emotions, or personal relationships. They think: "Everyone is out to get me. I must get them before they get me." It's all a game of power.

The lives of such bosses are dominated by fear, envy, jealousies, back-stabbing, hyper-competitiveness, and their pride of professional success. Men and women of this description inevitably are materialists. They are willing to do anything, anytime and anywhere, in order to get ahead, not minding the amount of pain or hurt which they may inflict upon their co-workers. They possess a sadistic mentality about work.

Such bosses as described above pay close attention to office gossips and, if they happen to be the C.E.O.'s, set-up spies to spy on their fellow workers to try to dig up dirt on them. They do not care about your right to privacy and freedom of expression. You may ask me: "But, how do you know these things?" Friend, I was not born yesterday.

In the five decades of my life, I have observed much about people. My undergraduate area of interest was personnel management. I specialize in observing human beings. I was a civil servant for ten years. I took notice of office rivalries, setbacks, and office politics.

I have observed and known of many supervisors who would not fairly recommend their juniors because of their own personal psychological and emotional inadequacies. It is a sad aspect of our human experience. Any honest and hardworking employee can face some of these kinds of experiences. And the annoying habits of your boss or supervisor can lead you into insanity if you let him or her.

Let me be specific with some examples. Sam was a snob nondescript from Nigeria. In the 1970's, he traveled abroad to study and returned to Nigeria with a Master of Science degree. Soon, he became the head of a government department there. If you were the first person in the morning to meet Sam at work, he would not respond to your greeting. I used to wonder what happened to him when he was abroad.

Then, in 1980, I had the opportunity to travel to the United States for further study myself. Before leaving Nigeria, I applied for study leave with pay from the government so that I could sponsor my education. The reply and approval was long in coming. I arrived in the United States and kept on corresponding with the department where I had worked, hoping that the approval to my application would be forthcoming. It never came.

I was frustrated and nearly stranded. But when, out of anger and dejection, I wrote to Sam that I was resigning, he forwarded to me the government's approval for the leave. Unfortunately, it was too late. The approval period for me to accept the offer had expired because Sam had suppressed the information from reaching me on time.

Another example of an extremely domineering, controlling personality that I had to deal with occurred at Howard University in the 1980's when I was a doctoral student. A black woman named Genna arrived to become the head of our department just when I was completing the program in history. Suddenly, she took away the scholarships which the university had provided for me. I was left to face a financial crisis of not having enough money with which to complete the program or to raise my new family.

I appealed to Genna for a lecturer position which, in the past, had been granted to All But Dissertation (A. B.

D.'s) in the department. She denied my request. Then, I appealed to one of the Deans of Social Sciences who graciously sympathized with my plight and assisted in obtaining the lecturer position for me. Then my real problems with Genna began!

She started to harass me by demanding that I wipe the chalkboard after the class lectures, that I pick up all the trash from the floors left behind by students in my classes, and that I arrange the chairs in those classrooms. She would appear in my classes without warning and sit in there to monitor my teaching. Even the students began to complain about her interference and intrusions.

It was an awkward and difficult situation which made it a very uncomfortable environment to teach. I would come to class in tears. She was new to the university and I had had no disputes or any interactions with her before all this happened. I wondered whether she mistreated me because I was a foreigner. When I protested that her administrative actions were making things difficult and pointed out that no other faculty had ever been made to do the kinds of things which she demanded of me, and that she was asking me to be a janitor instead of a lecturer, Genna threatened to "discipline" me.

She went right ahead to place queries in my student records and personnel file. As a result of her harrassment, I resigned my position as a lecturer. She forced me out of the only source of income which I had at the time. She knew that I was a foreign student and, therefore, had nowhere else to go.

Our relationship totally broke down when I discovered that Genna had also written official letters to the university authorities requesting that I should never be awarded the Ph.D. for which I had invested more than seven years full-time! Her request ignored the fact that I was an excellent student with a high G.P.A.

Nobody on the faculty came to my rescue. There was a conspiracy of silence and inaction by all. Genna also ignored standard faculty grievance procedures, but who cared? I was a powerless, foreign student. Therefore, I sought legal assistance which did help me to finally receive the Ph.D. Genna's bossy style cost me a huge debt by way of legal fees. She was really a boss!

In my professional career, I have known some heads of divisions or departments who are intimidated by hardworking and productive colleagues. If you find yourself writing and publishing more books and articles than your head of department does, you may be in for trouble. Instead of being praised and encouraged, you may actually be fired, yes, fired by your boss for some bizarre reasons or for no reason at all.

Also, I know of some faculty people who fraternize with students in order to obtain some sexual favors and they actually do reward such students with good grades. There are others who socialize with students and administration officials in order to be popular and keep jobs and tenure. Truth has been paying a terrible price within the academe.

These are the "yes boys and ladies" to the college presidents, heads of departments, and administration officials. At one Southern black college, a faculty member was caught with his pants down making out with a female student in the administration block, in a room not far off from the president's office! But the president had the reputation of running the institution like a plantation.

At this college, there were reports of spying on faculty and reporting incidents to the president. Some of my colleagues warned me never to speak my mind on anything at the faculty meetings if I intended to keep my job. I was shocked to discover the level of autocracy at this college in a country known for its democratic principles and academic freedom.

Believe me, some of the cruelest people that I have had the unfortunate luck of meeting in my life are the Ph.D.'s who use their pen to destroy other people. Nobody wants to talk about these things but I am bringing them out in the open since we are dealing with bosses who make you sick.

And what do you think is at the root of the sexual harassment at the workplace? Is it friendship and respect for the one harassed? Obviously not. Sexual harassment is often due to the abuse of power and it is often intended for the satisfaction of the libido of the harasser. And, let me state categorically that sexual harassment is not a male thing.

There are many men silently suffering from sexual harassments from women coworkers or female bosses because it is a no-win situation in these days of women's liberation for a man to complain about sexual harassment. Female students have been known to blackmail or even threaten male faculty with sexual harassment charges if they do not receive good grades.

On several college and university campuses in America, a male faculty member who is accused of sexual harassment is instantly deemed to be guilty. The accusation is by itself enough reason for dismissal and for the ruination of one's career. Many a male faculty walks a thin line between total submission to an unruly boss and being accused of or set up for sexual harassment charges.

One thing is clear: a person who sexually harasses someone is not a friend of the one harassed. It's all about power game-playing and the erotic element. And, of course, the authoritarian boss is not practicing a friendship relationship.

Many employees in the workplace face the possibility of exploitation over their pay and benefits' entitlement. Solomon is a friend of mine who works for a particular health-care agency in Washington, D.C. He had applied to work at this company as a manager. Instead, he was employed, not as a manager, but in a lesser position. Solomon went through a successful interview with a female boss but months later, to his utter amazement, he was receiving half the pay for the hours he had worked.

Solomon had put in seventy hours of work but received half the pay he should have received. When he complained, the authorities there began to give him the run-around. He approached me for advice and I told him to stand his ground and be ready for a court battle. Eventually, he was paid the balance but his female boss had used intimidating tactics to try to deprive Solomon of his due pay.

Sometimes, it is not only the monetary exploitations which many employees are subjected to. Often, an employee who is faced with an authoritarian boss and falls into his or her disfavor can suffer from some unfounded malicious slander or libel. Office gossip can erupt resulting in dangerous rumors. The employee may thus be set up for an improper and heartless firing.

All these things do happen at the workplace where the conventional wisdom is that one must try to get ahead by all means necessary. The basic work ethic at this sort of place is that the end justifies the means. But, indeed, there is need for all of us to retreat from this conventional attitude in the workplace. There is a better way -- the way of friendship.

## Return to Work Friendship

Nathaniel Stewart, who wrote the book, *Winning Friends at Work* in 1985, strongly believes that friends on the job can mean success on the job. But he warns that friendships at work do not just happen. Believing also that relationships at work can also be satisfying personally and professionally, Stewart suggested the ways we can choose friends at work.

Stewart also includes abundant information about the ways to weather the storms at work. Like Block and Greenberg, he insists that work and friendship *can* mix. Co-workers *can* be our best and cherished friends, especially considering we usually spend more time with them (40 hours a week) than almost anyone else in our life, except, perhaps, our immediate family.

He explains first why the average person works in order to lay a background for our understanding of this kind of friendship. According to Stewart, there are ten reasons why people engage in any occupation. That include: to have security, to fulfill one's ego, for social values, to lead a more purposeful life, to satisfy the feeling of personal progress, and to maintain one's identity in a culture in which a career or profession defines one's identity.

Moreover, we work in order to break out of the poverty cycle, to possess a new lifestyle, for the desire for more power, and in order to apply our educational training in concrete ways. These are all good reasons to work. But there also some bad reasons.

Stewart said that there are four bad reasons to work: the release of one's frustrations, the satisfaction that one gets for having aroused conflicts at the workplace, the venting of violent emotional tensions, and the acquisition of power, domination, and control of the lives of other coworkers. One can either use the opportunity to work to enhance good relations at work, or for the destruction of healthy relationships in any occupation.

He identified over ten kinds of friendships, namely:

- Commuter friends
- Mutual interest friends
- Luncheon friends
- Conference/meeting friends
- Travel friends
- Union friends
- The clique
- The Mentor
- Collaborative friends
- Personal friends.[5]

He focused on the last two which he termed "the two most significant and rewarding work friendships."[6]

The emergence of these kinds of friendships, Stewart said, may be instantaneous or they may grow slowly over time. But these friendships do exist. He said that "the most important feature of the [work] friendship is that your personal concerns off the job and your occupational problems on the job are intertwined, and the impact of these problems is shared."[7]

What makes work friendship so special is that this friend is someone *you* choose because he or she appeals to you and shares a large part of your occupational or professional or career concerns. This friendship is characterized by a recognition of each other's skills and talents, a mutual concern for each other, and a readiness and willingness to protect each other's individuality, reputation, and dignity by keeping things confidential between the two friends.[8]

Stewart then examined the nature of this work friendship and stated that the five main qualities of such friendships are empathy, discretion, ethical conduct, organizational intelligence, and emotional maturity.[9] Chapter Five of his book is devoted entirely to an analysis of how to choose a friend at work.[10]

He concludes that there are rewards to be gained from work friendships. Among these are happiness, the minimization of errors, learning from the team, networking, mutual support in coping with one's workload, improved communication and an enriched lifestyle.[11] Thus, it is obvious, at least from the point of view of Nathaniel Stewart, that winning and making friends at the workplace can be a vital, rewarding experience.

## Examples of Work Friends

We have thus seen that work friendships are possible. Let us examine some specific cases. Here, we find that *individuals can* mix friendships with work. Also, there are some *corporations* and *organizations* which, by their very nature, enhance friendships at the workplace. We should analyze these two possibilities. Let us begin with the individual, personal cases.

In her book, *Friends As Family*, Karen Lindsey discusses four individuals who had introduced the concept of friendship into their occupations. Jane was over forty years old and a therapist who counseled broken families. Francis was also a therapist but a homosexual male. Anita was both a therapist and a college professor who supervised a group of graduate students doing their masters' theses on friendship for two consecutive years.

She was a lesbian feminist.

Mel King was a black Bostonian civil rights male activist, a state representative, and a community organizer with an office at MIT.[12] These four persons had mixed friendship with work and found that friendship enhanced their success. After over twenty years of marriage, Jane separated from Michael, her husband. From this experience, Jane began to introduce to her clients in a group therapy the idea of friends who can become one's own family.

She would match up persons with similar family origins and backgrounds, believing that persons with common interests and backgrounds were likely to talk freely with one another. "So when we're talking about a therapy group becoming a chosen family, we're talking overtly about the kind of matching that people are probably going to find the most useful.[13]

In her counseling sessions with women, Jane encouraged "them to work with their friends who are family in that way."[14]   Although she had ended her marriage with Michael, Jane was still bonded to him as she kept a friendship relationship with him. Even though they had separated, they had not gotten a formal divorce up to this point.

Jane said that she had observed that friendships did not always evolve into successful marital relationships. But friends were important to her as members of a new family of separated women. And such friends included the ones she made at work.

Francis believed that "the extended family isn't just the people I'm living with, but friends that I've met ..." Also in his forties, Francis tried "to cement networks" among the gay community where he worked. He told them:

" You're here together, you should be here for each other.

It's beginning to work that way in one of the groups."[15]

For Anita, hers was a personal concern about creating "familial friendship networks." She assisted her students in conducting surveys on friendships and used the information in "friendship network as a reconceptualization of the family."[16] Although a lesbian, Anita included men in her own network.

She said: "Part of my whole agenda is trying to get people to be more conscious of their friendships. Our attitudes have really been that friends just come and go.... Mostly when I think of friends and friendship networks I'm thinking in terms of gratification, need meeting. That's what a family is about -- meeting each other's social, psychological, emotional needs. And I'd go so far as to say that the majority of those needs are really met by friends."[17] So, we find here that Anita is applying her idea of friendship to her classroom lectures and tutoring.

In Mel King's case, the idea of "kinfolk" is incorporated into community activism. His idea embraces a broader concept of the family. Mel King had observed that "folks don't even know the people in their apartment buildings."[18] From this simple observation, King determined to build a community out of working people -- a family out of the community.

Lindsey writes that "Mel King has been able to create new kinds of familial networks that challenge the rigid boundaries set up between family member and neighbor, neighbor and friend." For him, "family is a flowing and changeable, adaptable concept."[19]

Although I do *not* approve of Lindsey's lesbian lifestyle, I must stress that the so-called "straight" people ought to do what Lindsey has advocated, namely, to embrace more and more people into the circles of the traditional family and to treat such people as real friends.

This is the main message that I hope this book will convey to its readers.

Especially for a Christian, it is the scandal of our religious calling that we do not often embrace the notion of friendship into our religious faith. The Good Samaritan evidently saw the stricken fellow as his neighbor and friend in a broader sense. This, I believe, is what Jesus meant to teach. Elsewhere, he pointedly rebuked his disciples by saying that he who was not against them was on the Lord's side (Luke 9: 49-50).

Jesus had a broader view of family. His view included the extension of the hand of friendship to all with whom he came into contact. Except for Judas Iscariot, the twelve men who worked with Jesus turned out to be his most ardent friends and disciples. Ten of them were martyred because of their relationship with him.

Block and Greenberg cited a 35-year-old woman lawyer who said: "My family is far away, my lovers çome and go, but my friends seem to remain forever. I depend on my friends to help me in times of crisis today the way I depended on my family when I was growing up. I could not survive without them, nor would I ever try to."[20] Obviously, her friends included persons in her legal profession.

Madeline, another 36-year-old teacher, found other teachers at work as friends. And they were not in "competitive situations."[21] Block and Greenberg found other women in several occupations whom they interviewed and who proved that friendship at the workplace was possible. Madeline's case reminds me of my teaching years at the high schools in Nigeria.

The Nigerian Civil War was looming in the horizon. I had graduated in 1966 from high school. My first job as a teacher was at my alma mater, Nsit Peoples' Grammar

School at Afaha Obio-Offiong. Later, I got another job at Methodist Secondary School, at Odot, in the present Akwa Ibom State of Nigeria.

Except for the principal, many of the teachers I worked with including myself lived in mud and wattle-walled houses with thatched roofs. Our lives were very intertwined with each other. I recall nothing of the competitiveness rampant in the Western business culture. We were like brothers and sisters caring for the students under our ward.

Sometimes, we shared meals with each other. It was like we were living in a monastery without the ascetic lifestyle characteristic of that type of institution. I long for some of those years and wish I could visit some of those colleagues again who made my earliest professional life meaningful. S. K. Okpo will forever be missed for his fatherly role as my principal at Odot.

When I joined the civil service around 1971, I came into contact with E. I. Eteng from the Obubra district of the Cross River State of Nigeria. He was one of my senior officers. He stood out as a dignified, kind, gentle and honest co-worker friend. He was the type of boss you wished you had as a beginner in any career -- empathic, caring and understanding. He was also Sam's colleague whom I earlier referred to in this chapter. Eteng was different -- he was not a snob.

In the years that I have taught in the American colleges and universities, I have met people like Nancy, Lenny, Ampiaw, and Ekpo who qualify as co-worker friends. I met them as faculty members in a particular southern college. Although my time at that college was only a few months, I felt like I lost great friends on the day I departed.

I will not forget the spiritual upliftment which I

received through a visit by Ampiaw who reminded me, in his humorous manner of saying things, that "all things work together for the good of them that love God." These words were indelibly impressed upon my heart.

Lenny was particularly unique in his empathic expressions and actions. He fought in defense of my interests. He took me out three times to eat and talk. He linked me up with the United Nations Association where I socialized.

Above all, he made me re-believe in myself -- that I was still professionally significant at a time when the head of division attempted to destroy my self-esteem and my family income. And, Lenny is white. In America, this fact makes our friendship even much more significant, given the racial climate of the country. Lenny, if you read this, I really miss you. The world needs more friends like you.

## Corporations Enhancing Friendship

Karen Lindsey, whom I mentioned earlier in this chapter, believes that there are *organizations* and *corporations* which, by their structure, help bring people together into a meaningful relationship. These organizations and corporations may be religious, social, political, or economic. They may even be governmental.

Lindsey cited one such agency -- ACTION -- a sponsor of the Foster Grandparent Program, which enabled nearly 17,000 low-income elderly people to become paid "grandparents" to children with special needs.[22] It is not like the government paid these workers to be friends with needy people. But their labor enhances the chances of building friendships while at work.

Some other health-care agencies and programs also fall

into this category. These workers are never fully and adequately compensated for their labors. Nevertheless, many of these workers do so because of the non--monetary blessings which they derive at work. Some volunteer-corps agencies may be included here, too.

In some communities, the YMCA and the YWCA, the Boys' and Girls' Scouts clubs, the Red Cross Society, and some other volunteer firefighters' organizations offer opportunities for the promotion of real friendships. The Big Brother/Big Sister groups, the Fellowship of Christian Athletes, the Christian Pilots Associations and the Christian Medical Association offer the same opportunities.

I mentioned my daughter's involvement with the missionettes in our current church. This program does foster meaningful friendships if run properly. Some other churches have visitation programs through which their members regularly visit the neglected, the sick, and the needy. The members then report back to their church leaders. And friendships do arise from such religious activities.

Friendship activities have ways of impacting directly or indirectly upon the corporate sins and the structural evils of our society. A man with any moral consciousness and, particularly, a Christian, can well remember that Daniel was a godly worker whose influence as an excellent civil servant had an impact on the destiny of an empire.

The challenge before us today is to rediscover the Daniel spirit within each of us who can become friends with others in the workplace. It is in this manner that we can become the Sons of God (S.O.G.), the sons of light, beaming our radiance of true friendship to those in search of friendships in the workplace.

# CHAPTER EIGHT

# FRIENDSHIP AT CHURCH

*Blessed are they who have the gift of making friends, for it is one of God's best gifts.*

--- Thomas Hughes

*Friendship cannot become permanent unless it becomes spiritual.*

--- Hugh Black

I love the theme song of the television program, "Cheers." One of the lines of this song says: "Sometimes, you wanna go where everybody knows your name." It reminds me of one reason why I go to church. Among many, one of the reasons I go to church is to be where somebody knows my name -- to be among friends. To be sure, there is a spiritual reason for going to church. But there is also a social reason. Making friendships at church is one such reason, isn't it?

James Osterhaus, already referred to in this book, writes that "the Bible is a book about friendships."[1] If the preoccupation of the churches is with the Bible and the Bible is about friendships, should one not expect that the Church ought to be the one place where friendships are made? But, quite frankly, this is often not the case. One of the troubling aspects of modern American life is the near absence of genuine friendships in the church community. If you have not yet realized it, church people can be and are often friendless and lonely, too.

## Noisy Assembly, Friendless People

At the average 11:00 o'clock morning service at a local church, the congregation is involved in worship, making a joyful noise unto the Lord. A spectator might think that this assembly is composed largely of very friendly people. But beneath this moment of *worship*, is often a superficial layer of interpersonal relationships. A spectator ought to wait in the parking lot to listen and evaluate what these worshippers say and do immediately after worship.

In September 1997, an article by Cathy Lechner in the Christian magazine, *Charisma*, amounted to a scathing indictment of the superficiality in church relationships. She wrote: "As much as I chafe when a friend tries to pull me out of my misery, I realize the value of having wonderful friends, and I do have several. These are people who are real with me, *not the type of people you often meet at church. Many Christians cannot sustain any type of meaningful relationship with other Christians. Their relationships are all superficial.*"[2]

Now, before you scream at her for generalizing, read this next observation. Stephen R Covey who, in 1989, published the number one national bestseller, *The 7 Habits of Highly Effective People*, also noted that church relationships can be superficial. He wrote that he believed "almost anyone who is seriously involved in any church will recognize that churchgoing is not synonymous with personal spirituality."[3]

"There are some people," he said, "who get so busy in church worship and projects that they become insensitive to the pressing human needs that surround them."[4] Covey himself had participated in organized church and community service groups throughout his life. Thus, he was not commenting as an outsider but as an insider. He pointed to a fact, not always reckoned with by churchgoers, that "you can be active in a church but inactive in its gospel."[5]

Like Lechner, Covey observed that "church-centered people often tend to live in compartments, acting and thinking and feeling in certain ways on the Sabbath and in totally different ways on weekdays."[6] Covey offered this insight: "Because the church is a formal organization made up of policies, programs, practices, and people, it cannot by itself give a person any deep, permanent security or sense of intrinsic worth. Living the principles taught by the church can do this, but the organization alone cannot."[7]

This evaluation of the church flies in the face of many clerics who think, believe, and act as though the Church is a divine institution directed by men. Such clerics forget that the Church is also a social institution where men and women flock to in search of deep, lasting and genuine relationships in the form of friendships.

There is yet another painful and disappointing

example of the superficiality in church relationships. This is pointed out by Osterhaus. According to him, Lyman Coleman was a church consultant who had met with 18 elders of a Presbyterian church several years ago. Coleman had posed a question to them regarding who was their closest friend, a person that each of them could call at 3:00 o'clock in the morning if they found themselves in urgent need, difficulty, or emergency.

This is what Coleman discovered: "Tragically, none of the elders had mentioned anyone in the church where they served, let alone anyone on the elder board who was seated in the circle."[8] Those 18 elders could not even call their own minister because they had no intimate relationships or friendships within their own church circle! Is this example unique among Presbyterians alone? I doubt it. How different this is from the lifestyle Jesus had with his disciples.

Jacqueline Olds, Richard Schwartz and Harriet Webster, the authors of *Overcoming Loneliness In Everyday Life* (1996) warned: "But remember always that joining a religious institution or any other organization simply for the social dividend seldom proves to be a fruitful path. Unless you are committed to the broader mission of the organization, you are likely to find the relationships you form within it as tenuous as your belief in the ideals the group represents."[9] This characterization calls for serious reflection by those who are proud to regard themselves as men of the cloth.

## Vibrant Organism, Weak Organization

A church can be a vibrant organism but nonetheless a weak organization. This is because, as has been stated before, churches are composed of fallible human beings.

The spirit may at times be alive but the structure may be weak or even sick. I do not mean that there are no redeeming aspects of the Church. As an organism solely directed by the Holy Spirit, surely there are redemptive benefits for the churchgoer. We shall see these later.

Any human institution, however, may be vibrant but certainly not flawless. I truly believe that from my research there are, in fact, millions of very lonely and friendless churchgoers around the world. They just haven't been discovered! This is particularly true in many of the so-called mega-churches where membership can reach up to 20,000 in one local assembly.[10]

I know one person who attended one of these mega-churches and who eventually left that church and began attending a smaller church. I had asked him why he left the large church in Washington, D.C. His reply? "I was only a number, a mere statistic. I felt that no one cared. The ministers were inaccessible. You had to make appointments in order to see the senior pastor. Sometimes, you had to wait for a long, long time or turn to one of his associates. The entire thing seemed like a corporation."

Brenda is another woman that I know of who had attended a mega-church in Baltimore, Maryland, for about 20 years. In all those years, she says, she never developed many intimate friendships at her church. A new pastor assumed the pastorate. Brenda describes him as an acquaintance, not a friend.[11] I wonder if many people in Brenda's church do feel the same way.

Unfortunately, it is not only the parishioners who are suffering from church-related friendlessness. There are unbelievably many pastors and their families, doing God's work, who are lonely, burned out, friendless and disappointed. Many divorces among pastors are due to these experiences. Terry Mattingly who teaches communications at Milligan College in Tennessee writes in a recent article about Jim Dahlman who reported that there are many pastors who live with an "overwhelming sense of loneliness and isolation."

These pastors confessed that they were "totally alone. We can't talk to anyone about what's going on in our lives or the pressure we're under. We're out here twisting in the wind." This sad admission reminds me of Chuck Swindoll who, in 1985, stated that "top dogs are loners," implying that high corporate executives as well as church officials can be lonely. After all, clergymen are human beings who desire friendships, too.

Believe me, I have also been around church people for over 25 years. In the individualistic-oriented American life, church life is supposed to be a private, personal matter. Those who deny this should explain to us why Walter Rauschenbush was severely criticized at the turn of this century by some ultra-conservatives when he introduced the "social gospel." I fail to see how anyone can deny the presence of friendliness in many churches.

In America, a church attendee often begins by shopping around. One may assume that he or she will be welcome at the first visit to a church. No doubt, nearly all the churches have a welcome ceremony during the worship hour. But do not be fooled by this first impression. Beyond this point, there may be much more to be desired than actually exists as far as caring members. George Barna, the founder and president of the Barna Research Group Ltd., knows something about this "church selection strategy."

Author of the book, *Finding a Church You Can Call Home* (1992), Barna describes "the church shopping excursion" experiences of many Americans. For 12 years,

Barna visited dozens of American churches to capture the vast array of impressions and insights which he gained from the exposure. Then, he conducted extensive national research among both lay people and clergy "to better understand what other people's experiences, expectations and desires have been in selecting a church."[12]

Barna wrote his book to provide information as to what other people found when they shopped for a church, the right kind of church, for themselves. He disclosed that from his findings, nearly 100 million Americans had been engaging in church shopping. After two years of committed attendance, financial support, and other involvement in a particular church, Barna and his family decided to quit their church. It had not been the right church for them.

Everything in their church outwardly seemed right. But still Barna felt a void within himself. "In my heart I desperately wanted a family of Christian people," he wrote, "with whom I could worship, communicate, volunteer my energies and study the Word of God. If the church I was attending did not facilitate that experience, then it was my responsibility to rectify the situation."[13] Barna changed churches five times over a five or six year period. Eventually, he did find a church where he and his family felt a peace worshipping and serving God. His book provides the guidelines for church shopping.[14]

The sickening aspect of this maddening process is that one has to shop for a church. Think of it. The one place on earth you might assume that you'd be fine may become your waterloo. You have to beware or you could be taken for a ride by church cons. There are other sickening aspects of church life that can impair the development of genuine friendships. I think of the race and racial issues afflicting the churches.

It is very possible for one to still go to a church in America and discover that you are not welcome because of the color of your skin. Many American churches are still racially segregated.[15] At one Southern Baptist church not too long ago, some African foreign students went to an all-white church to worship. They were approached at the gate and politely informed that there was a black church down the road. Such students have to shop around for not only the right church but also one that is not prejudiced against other races.

A person should not take for granted that churches are public places open for worship to anyone. This would be naiveté at its best. After the initial welcome ceremony, an attendee may soon discover the reality: the minister's handshake is all they will get. There may be no other follow-up calls to his or her home and he or she may need to make more than one or two or even three visits before anyone in the church appreciates his interest in the local assembly.

The average Christian church in the United States does not make home visits to newcomers. It is very sad that the Mormons and the Jehovah Witnesses do a far better job in this regard! One's decision to join a particular church often depends upon that first impression made during church shopping. But many clergymen do not realize how important visits to the home of church visitors is to the growth and expansion of their work and churches.

In my travels and having resided in several states like Ohio, Texas, Louisiana, Florida, Maryland, and the city of Washington, D. C., I have observed that many churchgoers are friendless and frustrated. Contrary to popular belief, the churches have not been successful in offering true and genuine friendships to people who walk through their doors.

Some churches have even had occasions for a brawl and the police had to be invited. Many people have left churches feeling bitter because of the hypocrisy of their leaders. Such people ought to be encouraged that there are possibilities for friendships within the Church.

Perhaps, now we should ask the question, "why do so many churches fail at providing the opportunities for genuine friendships for their members?" As we have seen, Stephen Covey gave an obvious answer. But there are other reasons responsible for failure in the growth of church friendships. These include: leadership insensitivity, distorted worldview, narrow-mindedness, the structures and organization of the local assembly or denomination, the nature of and emphasis on programs rather than on character, and virtues development.

Also, there is the cultural problem. Americans are prone to saying on a Sunday morning: "I'm wonderful and great, thank you," when asked how they feel. The answer is usually not the whole truth. They conveniently leave out the near-fatal battle they had had with their spouses or family members before going to church that very morning. Those who engage in these practices are phoney and newcomers to their churches soon discover their lies.

Dr. Harold C. Warlick, Jr., a Southern Baptist minister, offered another clue as to why friendship promotion has failed in the churches. In his book, *Conquering Loneliness*, he explains that "often the Christian churches become as regimented as secular institutions."[16] He adds that "protestant competitiveness cause many ministers to view human beings as plums to be picked or scalps to be taken in the upbuilding of the institution."[17]

He says that one pastor told him that "his large parish had to 'take in' over five hundred new members a year to simply 'break even'."[18]   Other pastors told Warlick that their churches had become so big that they could no longer call their members by name.  It is no wonder that relationships have become superficial and phoney. Warlick maintains that it seems that "in many instances religious display can become a symptom instead of a cure for loneliness."[19]   One can say the same thing about church-related friendlessness.

We should not forget that in capitalist America, churches are big business. According to Dr. David B. Barrett, a research professor of Missiometrics at Regent University, in Virginia Beach, Virginia, the income of the Christian churches in the United States in 1997 was estimated at $95 billion.  Giving to Christian causes stood at $200 billion.  Barrett projected that the former will reach $100 billion by the year 2,000 and the latter $220 billion.[20]

This megabucks mentality does have an impact upon the clergyman whose ambition is to avail to himself a piece of the American dream.  The influence which money can have on a clergyman, and so impede his prospect of providing spiritual friendship, is shown by the case of Jim Bakker of the PTL fame.

In his 1996 autobiography, Bakker admitted that "it was possible to be surrounded by people, to be immersed in activity, and still be unbearably lonely."[21]   Bakker disclosed that one of the things that went wrong at his Heritage USA (an enormous Christian retreat center and theme Park in North Carolina) was his obsession with building brick and mortar rather than with building men and their spirits.

He has discovered since then that big church buildings and programs are not synonymous with God's prosperity or his blessings upon his people. The bigness may just be due to the rapacious schemes of a leader. Bakker confessed that he was so consumed with building and expanding PTL and Heritage USA that he simply "ignored or purposely attempted to avoid the very people for whom Heritage USA existed."[22]

This mindset contributed greatly to Bakker ignoring the spiritual health and nourishment of the people around him. He also ignored his children. In fact, his obsession was partly responsible for the death of his marriage. He wrote: "We started out with the best of intentions and somehow got sidetracked onto a path of pride, arrogance, and indulgence. We got trapped in the subtle snare that says, 'big is better'."[23]

Also, and this is significant, Bakker ignored the warnings of many dear and good friends such as evangelist James Robinson and Jamie Buckingham. It wasn't until God slammed him behind prison bars in 1989, that he learned that one of the most tragic mistakes in his life was to allow his vision of Heritage USA to become the focal point of PTL rather than keeping the gospel of Jesus Christ as his top priority.[24]

Henceforth, Bakker would not emphasize the growth of the physical structures any longer, but would instead encourage people to fall in love with Jesus, the greatest friend there is. I personally met Bakker on July 2, 1997, during a Promise Keeper's rally at Evangel Church in Maryland. He was a changed man. He gave a powerful message titled "Bruised, Broken and Burned-out Brothers," choosing his text from Jeremiah 20:7. We were all blessed that night.

## Personal Experiences

I have written elsewhere about my own encounters with loneliness and friendlessness here in U. S. churches and colleges.[25]   I can recall now the many smiles and handshakes I received following my first-time visit to some churches. These were some of the most superficial experiences I have had. I always wondered whether I was wanted or not.

I am not claiming that all the smiles and handshakes were totally fake or pretentious. But, with hindsight, I can say that only a few of such smiles were sincere and genuine. Indeed, we live in a society where superficiality is laudable. Warlick warns us that no one should suppose that all churchgoers are the friendliest of human beings. He says: "The Church is a human community guided by God, and not a divine community guided by humans."[26]

## Spiritual Friendships

So far, I have been preparing you for the discussion which goes by various labels: "spiritual friendship," "friendship with God," "inspirational friendship," "divine friends," and a "theology of friendship."[27] Whatever the label, this is the kind of friendship which comes through our experiences with God and His Church.

We must not forget that, as an organism, the Church is still God's property which Jesus Christ inaugurated. The Church has a God-given mandate and responsibility to do far better than secular institutions can do in this area of human relationships, including the practice and promotion of true friendships.

Mistakes, errors, and flaws are bound to exist because the Church is also made up of fallible human beings.

But having said this, the mandate of the Church is still that she foster healthy relationships which buttress the fact that human identities and personhood are vitally important. A church which ceases to do this soon loses its significance.

Author Paula Riple, whose ministry was among separated and divorced Catholics, insists that the essence of Christianity is a call to friendship. She writes that "Christianity is based on the two great commandments which tell us that human beings can neither live nor grow in isolation. Without God's love we cannot discover who we are. Without the love and friendship of human companions we become less than we are."

She adds: "Of all the gifts that God gives to sustain and nourish our lives none can equal the presence of a faithful friend."[28] Riple points out that Jesus deliberately linked our love for God with our love for our neighbors. The most fundamental call of our faith, she asserts, is "a call to live as friends."[29] It was Jesus who declared: "You are my friends, if you do what I command" (Jn. 15: 14). And what did Jesus command us to do? To love one another as He had loved us.

Jesus went on to add: "Greater love had no man than this, that a man laid down his life for his friends" (Jn. 15: 13). Jesus loved us so much that he died for us. God so highly prized and loved us that he sent Jesus to teach us how to love God and our fellow man. We can be his friends if we accept his finished work on the cross. It is really an honor to be God's friend. Abraham was reputed as being God's friend. And remember, Abraham is claimed by Moslems, Jews, and Christians as their patriach. We ought to copy his example and stop fighting each other.

Here, we should note that love and friendship, as far as

Jesus was concerned, go hand in hand. The two are inseparable. Remember that Lillian Rubin tells us that friendship entails trust, honesty, respect, commitment, safety, support, generosity, loyalty, mutuality, constancy, understanding and acceptance. "These," she writes, "are the most widely heralded qualities of friendship, the minimum requirements, if you will, to be counted as a friend."[30] But notice that these traits are also the demands or expectations of a loving relationship.

It is possible to build friendships that point to God, as Timothy K. Jones has suggested in his book. Or, to find and develop a friendship with God, as both Floyd McClung and John W. Crossin have argued in their books. There is a theology of friendship which places God at the center of our lives. We can befriend God's presence, as John A. Payne, the Dominican priest has maintained. In all these respects, we are engaged in spiritual friendships with God and with our fellow man.

We can develop the most intimate relationship there can be both horizontally and laterally. It is, perhaps, in this sense that author Carmen L. Caltagirone sees friendship as a sacrament wherein we touch God and are touched by the lives of good and caring friends. No one can deny the richness of this kind of wonderful life. A minister of the gospel who deeply understands these dimensions of Christianity and applies these concepts to his theology does his congregation a world of good in fulfilling the trinitarian components of authentic Christianity. For, we are truly body, soul, and spirit.

Therefore, whether we pray, study God's word, share our testimonies with one another, or assist the needy, we should not do all these things just for ourselves, just to appease God (as though he needed to be appeased), or just to show off how godly we may be, but we do these things to fulfill God's original purpose -- to bring about divine fellowship with him and with one another.

I really believe that this, and the glory of God, are the ultimate purposes of our human existence. This is why I believe that a life of greed and selfishness is intolerable and reprehensible to God and society. It is friendship, spiritual friendship, which should be at the core of our relationships. In order for us to be truly happy and really satisfied, we must embrace this spiritual friendship.

In his book, *It's Time to be Bold,* Michael W. Smith, a popular songwriter and musician, writes about the importance of Christian friends and the place for Church in our lives. Insisting that "being a friend is the most natural way to influence people," he asserts that friendship "is God's favorite strategy for reaching the world with his love."[31] He writes that by listening, showing interest and empathy, we can reach the most supposedly *unreachable* person in our communities. Smith offers several reasons why Christian friends are important. According to him, they:

♦ lift us up and provide us with a clear perspective on life

♦ support us in our walk with God.

♦ love us enough to deflate us when the need arises and they build us up when we are down. They are our encouragers

♦ exhort us with God's word.

♦ act as role models for us. They make us want to be more of a godly person.

- challenge and inspire us to greater heights of spirituality. They hold us accountable since we need people who understand our problems and will still love us in spite of such problems.

- help us to be at home with ourselves. They are not there to judge nor condemn us. They are there to help us become better people.

- are the ones who can be brutally honest with us. They act as "spiritual watch-dogs" and remind us that we are capable of making very serious mistakes, particularly, if we are leaders. Such friends are invaluable.

- remind us that we can never make it alone; we were never meant to make it alone; and we shall never make it alone. We need their wisdom, insight, knowledge and talents to make it through a world of peer pressure.

But notice that these blessings of friendship are possible within the Church community.

Smith argues that the problem has been that churchgoers deviated from the original purposes and mission of the early Church. He writes that the real Church was about average people who loved God so much that they really wanted to learn how to love each other.[32] He insists that the Church was about the business of caring for "ex-cons, street-smart junkies, toothless old winos, pathetic vagrants, and the homeless such as Big Leon."

Also, Smith writes that the early Church was deeply interested in the plight of the poor, the hungry and the destitute. The true Church is much larger than a building or a program. The business of the Church is fully expressed in the manifesto of Luke 4:18. However, many modern churches today have sunk deep into nonsensical formalisms and churchianizing. Truly, some churches are irrelevant and proclaim dead sermons to spiritually dead people.

Many young people today declare that the church is irrelevant -- out of touch with them -- and does not care for them. In some churches, the pastoral staff seem not to care about the real needs of their members. Some church leaders believe and act as though man only has a spiritual problem.

Smith defines the Church simply as "a network of common people with common problems who really care for each other and want to share that same love with anyone else in need."[33] If the average church were of this sort, she would attract non-church people desperately in need of friendship and love.

Like Smith, I also believe in the Church, the real Church, the universal body of true believers. There is something about organized religion that is very troubling and of concern to me. This something is the violence that is characteristic of many modern religions. We must give the real Church a chance. We must remember that Christ loved the Church so much that he gave himself up for her (Eph. 5: 22). Christ did not die for the bricks and the organization which we call church. He died for the people -- living, human beings.

We are the people for whom Christ died. Clergymen should always keep this in mind. Therefore we, as Christians, cannot give up on the Church. If we do, we are giving up on ourselves. We are the temple of the Holy Spirit in whom God dwells. If God is really indwelling and working through us, then we can demonstrate his incarnation by being the true Church.

Think of how this dark world would have been without the redeeming graces of God working through His Church. Think of the many people who have been blessed by the Church -- the mini-Christs. I fully endorse Smith's proposal that we establish more home-fellowships, like those of the early Church, where we can build genuine friendships within the body of Christ.

In addition, I highly recommend that anyone in church leadership read a copy of Bakker's book, *I Was Wrong*. The mistakes which Bakker made are not peculiar nor unique. Every pastor or minister of the gospel is prone to the same temptations Bakker faced. We can learn from his experiences and not wait until God slams us behind bars. There is something in us, as leaders, which yearns for a large, larger, and constantly expanding successful ministry. The numbers' game is hardly escapable.

Therefore, parishioners must earnestly pray for their ministers to escape from ecclesiastical tyranny, pomp, and power. I mean the abuses of power within the local churches and denominations. And I believe it's extremely important for ministers to crush and break away from their religious cocoons, from their hermitic enclaves, and open up to the friendships which are available from their members. If only church leaders would imitate the humility of Christ and his openness and friendliness to all with whom he met. He who said: "Whosoever comes to me, I will in no wise cast out," was not a hermit.

## Some Practicals

Some practical things which I believe every church leader and his organization can do to promote genuine friendships are as follows:

### ◆ Know Your Members

Think of a corporate CEO who runs an organization but is not inclined to know the names of his board members and the key members of his company! Believe me, this kind of boss will not get very far. Yet, this is what many ministers are doing and hope to get away with. Every pastor or minister of the gospel must make a serious effort to know his members by name. This great responsibility goes with the territory.

The Church is not to be a giant corporation where each member is faceless or nameless. Many people who go to church are already associated with such "faceless" corporations in their careers. They come to church where somebody ought to know their names. This is important to the churchgoer. He or she wants, in fact, needs a church where the minister knows his or her name.

To be sure, growth and expansion can make it extremely difficult for the minister to know all his members by name. For a 20,000-member congregation, this is practically impossible. But there must be definite and clear steps taken to ensure that parishioners do not feel isolated, alienated, and everlastingly anonymous. A situation where this occurs would be counter-productive. A church is not a Fortune 500 company but should be a living organism where human beings count.

## ♦ Visit

Each church ought to devise an effective visitation program for members and for reaching people in the community. The churches should not always wait for sinners to come to church. But, as T. L. Osborn, a world famous evangelist said some years ago, Christians should be where the sinners are. A church visitation program should include trips to the prisons, hospitals, the zoos, the museums, recreational parks, sports stadia, and the streets. And why not? Are these not where the sinners are? Are these not the places where Jesus would have been found?

Churches should train their officials and members to know that God's work is for every believer and visitation is one channel through which the Christian can make himself visible to his community. It is a pathetic state when a believer feels that no one cares enough to visit him or her. The Christian is supposed to be his or her brother's keeper.

Love for the brethren includes house visitation. It is a shame when a pastor fails to visit the home of a member during the lifetime of his stay at a particular church locale. This says something about his motive in the ministry. To make friends with church members, a minister must visit his parishioners. He should keep an itinerary or log-book for this activity.

## ♦ Call Them Up

Thank God for the telephone. There is no excuse for a minister not to devise a plan for regular telephone calls to members of his church. I don't care how busy he may be. If he truly loves them, he would find that this calling is vital to his ministry. The problem is that most pastors do not realize how important it is for a member to receive a call, or better a visit, from his minister.

I know of some ministers who never make house visits or telephone calls. They are magisterially aloof and withdrawn. Quite frankly, the pastoral ministry is not for hermits or shy-ridden men and women who cannot enjoy the company of other people. The Bible commands us to be hospitable. By definition, a pastor is a shepherd, a fisher of men, a man or woman who loves association with other people for the Lord's sake.

Think of a fisherman who stays home waiting for some fish to visit. It is unthinkable or even ludicrous! But this is what most pastors do. A minister is bound by his profession to be, in the words of St. Paul, "all things for all men," including women. Regular telephone calls are a must. The minister ought to emulate the business industry and establish telemarketing-for-souls booths in his church.

The minister must engage all the hands in his congregation. In this way, he can convince his members and the community that he is accessible and really cares. These members would know that they are not isolated. Those ministers who feel the pressures of their calling too much for them to serve in these ways should leave the pastorate without shame.

### ♦ Be Just and Democratic

There are some church leaders who, like Jim Bakker, have allowed prominence and power to get into their heads *and they do not even realize it.* Such leaders often say that the church is not a democracy. They advance these misconceptions to rationalize their tyranny and autocracy. They do not often seem to understand that God is the only one who can claim a theocracy. Fallible human beings have never done very well with arbitrary or naked power. That is why governments have constitutions and the bill of rights. And, men, all men, must live by just laws and precepts.

Therefore, when a minister has become dictatorial, autocratic, and power-hungry, he is very likely to abuse his power and the fundamental human rights of his parishioners. We should never forget the Jim Jones affair in Guyana where the cult leader led his followers to commit suicide. Many churches have constitutions and bylaws. When a minister flagrantly and contemptuously disregards such constitutions and bylaws, and the best admonitions of his officials, he should be removed from office as a consequence. He has become intolerant, arrogant and abusive of the friendship requirements spelt out in this book. A tyrant is never a friend of freedom lovers.

### ◆ Love

Commitment to the simple message of love for Christ and his word and obedience to His word, remain the best weapons against the danger of regimentation in church polity. If this message is constantly and properly taught, a church can experience true revivals that lead to meaningful relationships among her members.

All churches should renew their commitment to the specification of love enunciated by St. Paul in his first letter to the Corinthians. The scriptures say that people will discern that we are really Christians by our love for one another. It is my heart's cry that the churches will rediscover the early Church's kind of love as she begins her journey into the 21st century.

### ♦ Pastors Are People Too

I have said some things which ministers can do to promote friendships in their churches. But I must also have some word for the worshippers. This is a word of caution, especially for the young and new believer. People need to realize that pastoring a church is usually a very difficult and challenging task, particularly, if the minister really cares and loves his people.

Many people think that a pastor is a lazy individual who works only on Sundays and does nothing on weekdays since he does not punch a time-clock, is often not supervised nor evaluated. This is erroneous thinking. As many pastors can testify, their work is often mingled with heartbreaks and frustrations. Ask any pastor who is unfortunate to head a church of elderly people and has to conduct funerals regularly without the presence of young people who marry and celebrate youth.

Therefore, the churchgoer must understand that ministers are human beings, too, and not angels. They also need parishioners' understanding, support and friendship. Their families and children need the love and appreciation of their parishioners. The Bible demands that we do not make their labors more difficult to bear.

### ♦ Pray

Before you severely and publicly criticize the minister, be sure you have earnestly prayed for him and have tried to befriend him or her. The rule: "do unto others as you would have others do unto you," is not applicable for pastors only. It is universal and for everyone. Pastoring is a difficult job which involves management and guidance of complex human beings.

If the average churchgoer understood the work of the pastor in this sense, he or she would not go to church expecting a single individual to take care of *all* the emotional, psychological, intellectual, social, economic and spiritual needs of the parishioners. In fact, some people expect a pastor to *cure* all their socio-economic and spiritual ills!

The believer, at all times, should endeavor to look to Christ first for solutions to all his or her problems. Sometimes, pastors condition the members to remain in a perpetual state of spiritual dependency on them so as to make it possible for the minister to rule over them. But a truly godly minister trains his people to be disciples, to be independent, to grow up in grace, to look to Christ, the author and finisher of their faith, to aim at maturity and be ready to serve Christ, their master.

A church should be a training ground for battle against the hosts of Satan. But in order to succeed, the churches must build strong friendships and loving relationships among the members. This is what is known as *koinonia*, and *diakonia* in theological terms. Church people can encourage and promote inter-family relations, home visits and fellowships, out-of-church excursions and field trips, all geared toward the enrichment of intimacy and friendships.

Church members should never wait for the pastor to initiate and participate in every such activity. They may seek his approval, but they should not be totally dependent upon him. The minister should never be jealous, envious and suspicious because he fears his power is eroding. He should not be that insecure. He should be a catalyst who sees to the general happiness and spiritual welfare of his flock.

In the end, society at large benefits from a church practicing friendships. Our nation and the world become better when the churches promote genuine intimacies and love. The churches must become a society of friends.

# CHAPTER NINE

# FRIENDSHIP AT SCHOOLS AND COLLEGES

*The ancients regarded friendship as the happiest and most fully human of all loves; the crown of life and the school of virtue. The modern world, in comparison, ignores it.*
— C. S. Lewis, *The Four Loves*

Friends don't kill friends. And, certainly, school and college friends would not kill their colleagues, right? Wrong. In the American school system in 1998, it was the killing season. Between February 19, 1997 and May 19, 1998, six different killing incidents occurred. The killings reflected the decrease in the importance of true and meaningful friendships in American society.

The popular media provided the following chronicle of these school-related killings:

### ◆ February 19, 1997

Evan Ramsey, 16 years old, killed his school principal and fellow student. He also wounded two others in Bethel, Alaska.

### ◆ October 1 , 1997

Luke Woodham, 16 years old, allegedly killed an ex-girlfriend, another student, and his mother (with a knife). He also wounded seven other students in Pearl, Mississippi.

### ◆ December 1, 1997

Michael Carneal, 14 years old, shot at a group of students, killing three and wounding five others in West Paducah, Kentucky.

### ◆ March 24, 1998

Mitchell Johnson, 13 years old, and Andrew Golden, 11 years old, at their Westside Middle School in Jonesboro, Arkansas, allegedly killed four students and their sixth-grade teacher, Shannon Wright. The other victims were Stephanie Johnson, Paige Ann Herring, Natalie Brooks, and Brittany Varner. The killers fired 27 bullets and injured 15 bodies that then lay  bleeding on the school's pavement.

### ◆ April 24, 1998

Andrew Wurst, 14 years old, opened fire at an eighth-grade school dance and killed a teacher in

Edinboro, Pennsylvania.

♦ **May 19, 1998**

Jacob Davis, 18 years old, allegedly killed a classmate in the school parking lot three days before graduation in Fayetteville, Tennessee.[1]

The most recent of these killings occurred at Thurston High School cafeteria in Springfield, Oregon during the last week of May 1998. There, Kipland Phillip Kinkel, 15 years old, coolly fired more than 50 rounds from a .22 caliber semiautomatic rifle among the 400 teenagers. Two boys, Ben Walker, 16 years old, and Mikael Nickolauson, 17 years old, were murdered.

Between 22 and 24 others were injured. Also, Kinkel allegedly killed his parents, William and Faith Kinkel, before the school cafeteria murders.[2] Could teenagers have done these terrible things to their own peers if any were real friends? Obviously not. It is not just at the high schools that these type of killings have occurred.

Crimes at 831 college campuses with more than 5,000 students each were surveyed and analyzed by *The Chronicle of Higher Education* The results released in April 1996 showed that in 1994 there were nineteen reported cases of college murders in the U. S. There were 1,509 cases of weapon violations. Drug arrests were on the rise.[3] One of these murders occurred at a place you and I would hardly expect it to happen -- Harvard University. The Harvard murder is the most heart-rending story that I have ever read. It shows how a failed relationship can turn into the most bizzare kind of human reactions.

In 1993, two young girls from two worlds apart were admitted into Harvard. One was Sinedu Tadesse from

Ethiopia. The other was Trang Ho from Vietnam. They were both considered "nice, petite, hardworking, foreign-born premed junior biology majors."[4] They were both brilliant and had come from reasonably well-to-do family backgrounds. Sinedu's family was of the Ethiopian Orthodox Church, whereas Trang's was of the Buddhist faith. They were both ambitious and dreamed of immense contributions to human society.

During their freshman year in 1993, they had become roommates. Sinedu had met Trang in a science class and she had become friendly with her. Sinedu even told her father that Trang was her best friend. But in the early hours of Sunday, May 28, 1995, Sinedu Tadesse stabbed Trang Ho forty-five times with a knife she had purchased for that purpose. She killed her roommate while Trang was asleep in her bed. Then she hung herself in the bathroom.

### Saturated Brains, Empty Hearts

The Harvard University incident reminds me of an occasion which I had with a student when I was teaching in Florida. In an informal conversation after class lectures one day, I had asked one of my students if she had any friends. Her reply stunned me. "I have friends but I don't need them," she had blurted out. That was on April 10, 1996.

But in the case of Sinedu she needed a friend badly. She thought she had found that friendship in Trang. She wanted her friendship so much that when she was rejected by Trang, Sinedu's world totally fell apart and crashed. She killed Trang in order to find the peace that her poor soul craved for. Sinedu is not alone. There are many of her kind in our schools and colleges. When they manifest themselves, we have tragedies.

American schools, colleges, and universities are filled with young men and women with saturated brains and empty hearts. As I will show, these young men and women are craving for something to fill a void which academic pursuits and attainment alone cannot offer. They are craving for love, fellowship, and meaningful and true friendships. They are crying out for fellowship -- for someone to reach out and touch them. But our school and college curricula are not structured to provide for such needs. We fill our young people with cranial knowledge but they are woefully destitute of divine wisdom.

Take, for instance, the case of the October 1, 1997, killings in Pearl, Mississippi. There, Luke Woodham is reported as saying: "I killed because people like me are mistreated everyday." In the case of the Jonesboro, Arkansas killings, reporters said that "many of the reputed perpetrators apparently felt like outsiders." Mitchell Johnson, one of the perpetrators, complained that his teacher, Shannon Wright, "was nice to everyone but him." Kipland Kinkel is reported to have stated that he killed his parents because they did not love him.

Although these statements are insufficient reasons or justifications for such horrific and barbarous actions, nevertheless they indicate to us what is wrong with our popular educational programs and goals. We no longer train people to be better human beings; we train them for the economic market. We simply do not care enough nor do we quickly respond to the crying needs from the desperate hearts of these loners.

Personally, I take offense at the statement attributed to a family member of the Kinkels who said: "Young Kip was just a bad seed." No, Kip was not a bad seed. He was a 15-year-old boy desperately in need of love and meaningful friendship which apparently neither the family, the school system, and/or the society took the time to provide.

God does not send us "bad seeds" to destroy us and break our hearts, unless the family member implies that young Kip was from the devil. But our Christian Bible does not teach us so. And we should remember that, according to media accounts, these killers were also the victims of unnecessary and frequent teases, ridicules, insults, and they angrily reacted to these societal problems. Some children can be very cruel to other children.

In the case of Mitchell Johnson, apparently he had not been taught how to handle rejection. His romantic interest in Candace Porter, an eleven-year-old fellow student, turned disastrous when he was rejected by her. Who is to be blamed: the parents, the school, or the society? What of the church? Where was the church when these children were toying with complicated matters like school-work and human affections?

Is anyone responsible at all, or were these children "free" to chart their own individual romantic courses and fulfillment? In any case, what is a 13-year-old boy doing getting serious with an 11-year-old girl? Did anyone care to tell them that they were too young to be entangled in such matters without proper parental supervision? [Though I can almost hear him scream, "It's my life and I'll do what I want."]

General Colin Powell, referring to these school-related tragedies, writes about "the safety net" which protected him when he was a young student. He makes the important point that he was not left to himself to decide on complicated matters like romantic love, school-work and friendship. Many American parents are too busy

pursuing their careers and are neglecting their children.
Powell says that his safety net included a host of family
members, relatives, neighbors, friends, and the church.

Powell remembers friends like Jay Sickser who offered
him his first job -- helping out at Sickser's store after
school. He recalls folks at the Young Men's Hebrew
Association who provided him with a place to spend time
in a secure environment after school hours. It does often
take a village to raise a child, as Hillary Clinton asserted
in her book by that title.

In my case, my parents ensured that I got back from
school on time to our home. They knew exactly at what
time school was over each day. They knew how long it
took for me to get home. I would have had to explain to
my father what I was doing along the way if I arrived
later than I ought to have arrived. And, of course, I would
have been disciplined if I was late.

There were also the assigned daily chores that I had to
do at home after school hours. These included running to
fetch water from the stream, going to the river to do
laundry, washing the dishes, going to the farm to assist
my parents, or selling foodstuff from house to house to
help out my mother. Early in life I was taught that the
devil finds work for idle hands! Children playing around
was a luxury my father could not afford.

The case of Sinedu is even more pathetic and tragic
when we realize that she was crying out at Harvard for
true and meaningful relationships which she admits she
never had. Melanie Thernstrom does an excellent work
in *The New Yorker* (1996) article when she reveals, though
indirectly, how the system failed Sinedu. Drawing a lot
from Sinedu's diary, Thernstrom confronts us with a
clear picture of a very troubled young loner being
tretched to deal with the realities of life in a strange and

unfamiliar environment.

We should remember that Sinedu was a foreign student struggling in a culture which was totally different from that which she was accustomed to. Only a foreign student who has been exposed to Sinedu's situation can really understand what she was wrestling with. Don't get me wrong. I am in no way excusing her killing Trang. After all, Trang was also a foreign student like her.

I, too, had been a foreign student and had been terribly lonely when I studied in Ohio and Texas. I would never think of jealously killing my roommate. In fact, one of my roommates had more friends than I did. He was more popular with African-American women. But I was more interested in my education and had less time for socializing. I badly needed my undergraduate and graduate diplomas.

Yet, from time to time, I experienced acute loneliness which was harsher during the holidays when most American students went home and I could not. So, I am sympathetic to Sinedu but, simultaneously, very sad about the tragedy which resulted from her inability to cope with her loneliness. Having said this, it is quite evident from Sinedu's diary that she faced a serious problem which the Harvard psychotherapists and authorities failed to appreciate.

It seems that high in the scale of priorities which Sinedu had was friendship, not premed education. In her high school yearbook, she had written that "friendship is one of life's most precious treasures." And it is. But most people care less about it until some necessity or tragedy strikes. It also appears that Sinedu's family did not realize how important relationships were to their daughter. Parents should learn from this.

She was sent away to a foreign land -- to the American

desert of loneliness -- where she felt isolated; where the weather was cold and her work was difficult; where "she was bewildered by American standards."[6] She became hyper-introvertish. And this is the juncture at which we find the conflict of two or three cultures intermingling in her life: one African, the other Asian, and the third, American.

Here are some excerpts from her diaries which reveal this conflict:

*I am desperate ... my life has been hellish ... Year after year, I became lonelier and lonelier... Then I cry when people forget about me, or dislike being with me ... for social life I had no one.*

*I am like a person who can't swim choking [sic] for life in a river. All you have to do is give me a hand and put into words what you already know. No expenses, no commitments or risks involved ... Please do not close the door in my face.[7]*

*I don't understand what people mean by the warmth of a family, the love of their mother and the security of their home. I grew up feeling lonely and cold amidst two parents and four siblings ... I spent very limited time with other families that it took me all my life to figure out what they had and what I did not have ...*

*There was a lot of emotional pain and trauma involved in my home life. My parents did not beat me or abuse me. They fed me, bought me clothes, sent me to good schools and wished the best for me. As a result I was unable to point at any tangible cause.*

> *Do not get me wrong, I do not blame them for all they did; they did not know how else to be.*[8]

When Sinedu found temporary relief in the friendship with Trang, she wrote:

> *The last four days were the highlight of my life thus far in Harvard ... my rooming problem was solved in the best possible way ... with a girl I would make the queen of my life. I could just see myself raising my head proudly whenever people ask me who I'm rooming with. I could see myself ... working hard to improve my life so as not to spoil the beautiful chance I'm given.* [10]

In these days when it is very popular to be a homosexual, it is easy and tempting for a Westerner to view Sinedu as a young girl bedeviled with feelings of lesbianism. But Thernstrom has taken care of that when she writes that Sinedu's diaries provide no direct mention of sexuality. In fact, she never shared her bed with Trang. Rather, it was Trang who did so with another friend, Thao Nguyen, who first witnessed the murder and vainly tried to save the life of Trang Ho.

In African and Asian societies, nothing here would suggest lesbianism. Such thinking would be the product of a Western mind-construct.[11] So, Sinedu was not a young African woman struggling to quell her sexual inhibitions or libido. She was genuinely searching for true friendship, was nearly obsessed with the thought that Trang was the embodiment of that friendship, and when she felt jilted and rejected, she planned and executed her friend's murder and then committed suicide.

Sinedu expressed the meaninglessness and frustration

in her life as she feared that she would not again be able to find another friend. Herein she was wrong. But she believed her worst fears. In her sophomore year diary she wrote that she was "on the way to depression and battered with pessimistic thoughts." Then she added:

> I am unlovable and a cuckoo ... Trang told me I am boring ... I felt like I'm boring her ... If I ever grow desperate enough to seek power and a fearful respect through killing, she would be the first one I would blow off ... I cry alone in the cold ... The bad way out I see is suicide and the good way out killing, savoring their fear and [then] suicide. [12]

Evidently, Sinedu had grown jealous and resentful of the family support which Trang received.

I believe that the boys mentioned earlier on in this chapter, had they been as old and articulate as Sinedu, would have revealed a similar desperation to have loving families, friends, and teachers who really cared. When Trang informed Sinedu that she [Trang] would be residing with two other girls the next year and not her, Therstrom reports that Sinedu "was devastated. She begged Trang to change her mind, following her out onto the streets and into the subway."[13]

Neither Trang, Nguyen, nor the Harvard authorities cared enough to realize how desperate Sinedu was. No one but Sinedu understood how important a real friend was to her. Even her pleading with Trang was misunderstood and was deemed as a sign of self-disrepect. Although Sinedu had been seeing Dr. Douglas Powell, a Harvard university therapist since her first year, no one took any particular interest in her condition.

Thernstrom states that "Dr. Powell didn't know

Sinedu very well," and adds: "It is hard to imagine how he could have failed to perceive her distress."[14] It is not hard for me to imagine because I know that, in American colleges and universities, most people do their work with an impersonal attitude. We are only doing our jobs without any personal involvement or concern.

The Mental Health Services at Harvard failed Sinedu. That explains why the officials there were extremely reluctant to speak to Thernstrom who comes from a Harvard family and who also graduated from Harvard. She was teaching English there in 1993. Sinedu had become a "floating" statistic which, in Harvardian terms, meant someone who nobody wanted to room with. And, I would not be extra hard on Dr. Powell nor on Harvard. For such is the state of many of the American schools, colleges, and universities.

As one who has taught at four different colleges and has observed the administrative maladies which a
freshman student has to go through during registration week, I am not unfamiliar with what Sinedu had to contend with. We can blame her all we want to but we would fain find the solutions which will ensure that there will be no other Trang Hos involved in the Sinedu kind of tragedies. A kind of *Animal Farm* politics has blinded the eyes and impaired the sensibilities of many on these college campuses.

I was very disappointed to read that Harvard says they were waiting for Sinedu to ask for help. My God! This poor soul was seeing one of the university's therapists since her first year. Harvard had refused to allow Trang to change her roommate when she feared for her safety with Sinedu. What else did they need to have as further evidence that Sinedu badly needed more and better help? I find the university's gag orders issued after the girls had died distasteful and ludicrous.

Therefore, I am inclined to believe that Trang died as a result of Harvard's negligence and failure to pay attention to her complaints when she had sensed some real hostilities from Sinedu. By refusing to allow Trang to take precautions when she feared for her life, Harvard bears some responsibility for the death of Trang Ho. The lesson here is that every parent who has a child at school or at a college should never take things for granted. They must constantly check out the safety nets for their children.

More information on the state of the schools and colleges in America shows that parents must beware. In 1996, a *News-Journal* report stated that, in the 1994 survey I mentioned earlier on, there were 1, 001 forcible sex offences, 1,375 robberies, 3,049 aggravated assaults, 19,172 burglaries, and 6,624 auto thefts on those 831 campuses that had been surveyed.[15]

Cameron Brett, a sophomore student at the University of Maine, died after intoxication and falling three stories from an attempt to climb to the roof of the Chi Delta Phi building at Bowdoin College. He had been partying at the fraternity house and he was only twenty years old.[16] Friends don't let friends drink and die in this fashion. And a school or college system that has the kind of statistics I have just cited should not be too proud of itself. For, obviously, it is not doing too much to produce better human beings.

## A Friendlier, Kindlier Education

I believe that the college campuses must stop being the breeding grounds for lonely, alienated and murderously inclined young people whose interests are in "freaknik" and socializing. Although it might be argued that the schools and colleges are just a reflection of the larger society, and this is quite undeniable, the purpose of good education, however, should be the betterment of the individual, not just the acquisition of skills and information to make a buck. Nothing more or less than this is required and it is required urgently.

The college where I received my undergraduate degree in Ohio thrived upon the reputation and motto of being "a college of persons." At Malone College in Canton, Ohio, the quality of the person(s) graduating mattered. This should be the case in all other institutions of learning. It is the quality of the person that should determine the success rate of the individual and not the amount of money that one makes.

Teachers should be very concerned about the quality of the persons who pass through their classrooms. Would we rather want to graduate more lonely, frustrated hatemongers and potential killers or more friendly, wholesome persons?

To educate, train, and produce quality graduates from our institutions will involve a radical departure and reconstructing of American education as suggested by some experts. For example, Michael B. Katz, a professor of history at the University of Pennsylvania, contends that the American institutions of higher learning are dominated by market principles.[17] In short, education is motivated by the economic factor. Money is the primary reason for acquiring an education. Otherwise, there would be no other necessary reasons for it.

This economic philosophy for educating Americans began when the institutions of learning departed from the traditional curriculum and philosophy of education -- one that embraced Christian faith and doctrine. In the 1850s,

Horace Mann spoke for those who would later advocate a values-free education. We have paid a terrible price for this kind of "enlightened" education.[18]

A friendlier, kindlier education is one which recognizes that the present form of training which we've offered to students at the institutions of learning is morally and spiritually inadequate. What motivates a young mind today when he or she is constantly told by secular scholars that to be a respectable intellectual demands being an atheistic? How can one find a basis for quality life when a religiously-minded scholar is constantly ridiculed by his or her peers as though his or her education was made suddenly inferior by his or her choice to embrace a particular faith?

As David E. Purpel has argued, our "education should serve primarily to facilitate the struggle for meaning; ... the key educational strategy is to nourish the critical and creative consciousness that will contribute to the creation and vitalization of a vision of meaning."[19] This vision of meaning would be one which includes both the moral and spiritual components of a good education which, in turn, becomes the basis for healthy relationships among educated people.

If the goal of popular education is directed toward crass materialism as an end and not as a means to an end, then we are seriously in deep trouble as a civilization. Therefore, we should not pretend ignorance as to why our college and university graduates are having moral crises on the campuses.

The place to begin this educational revivalism is at the elementary, junior and high schools, prior to college and university training. But, alas, unfortunately, our young people are no longer allowed to pray or receive religious instructions in schools. And, again, we are reaping the consequential fruits: teenage rebellions and confrontations, teenage pregnancies, violence and murders.

I am convinced that it would be very difficult for a teenager from a deeply spiritual home, one which practices the presence of God and the exercise of true Christian values, to walk into a school just before Thanksgiving and slaughter his fellow school mates. There may be some exceptional cases but the general rule is that spirituality has a restraining and moderating influence upon a young mind.

American educational policy-makers should reconsider this proposition just as the medical field is reconsidering the relationship between prayers, faith, physical health and medicine. The time for intolerable arrogance should be over. Are these policy makers not robbing some Americans of the experience of vital spiritual blessings which faith and knowledge would offer?

It is to be noted that *Time* magazine reported an important aspect relating to the West Paducah, Kentucky school killings. First, the magazine disclosed that fourteen-year-old Michael Carneal was a very troubled child. It appeared he had a lot of hatred. As one reporter put it, he had "pent-up frustrations that boiled over."[20] He had been teased all his life. But he had a friend, Benjamin Strong, whom he had warned not to be at the school's prayer circle that Monday. Benjamin was a senior at the school while Carneal was a freshman.

Benjamin refused the warning, however, and did hold and lead the scheduled prayer meeting on the day of the killings. The magazine says that "minutes before, at the prayer circle [of 35 members], Benjamin had seen Carneal enter the school lobby, and in his prayer he asked God for strength to last through the day."[21] As the Amen was said, the first shot was heard. Benjamin thought that Carneal had been shot. But when he saw that his friend, Carneal was doing the shooting, Benjamin forcefully ordered Carneal to put down the gun.

Carneal continued to shoot; the other students ran for cover; but Benjamin stood his ground and, for a third time, commanded Carneal to put down the gun. Eventually, he tackled Carneal, pushed him against the wall, causing the gun to fall to their feet. As far as I am concerned, Benjamin Strong, 17 years old, was the hero on that day. Now, let's ask ourselves some poignant questions.

Suppose that Benjamin had not prayed for strength -- would he have been courageous enough to perform the role that he did that day? Suppose that Benjamin had stayed away at home as Carneal had requested, how do we know that there would not have been more than three deaths? Suppose Carneal had joined the prayer circle that morning, would he have gone out from it to open fire upon his schoolmates?

We are told that Carneal never joined the prayer circle; he often only watched as they met. But suppose that Benjamin's influence upon Carneal had reached such a point whereby the troubled boy had become a Christian -- would he still have thought of massacring his colleagues? And, we should not ignore the fact (or the miracle) that Carneal's gun was still loaded when Benjamin ordered him to put it down. He could have killed Benjamin!

The miracle is that Carneal did not. He spared Benjamin's life. Those who assume that this was mere coincidence or good luck should think again the next time a killer is standing next to them and has his gun fully loaded. The citizens of Paducah seem to have sensed this miracle and have moved on to forgive the young killer by raising street signs to that effect. This is how to properly heal a community torn by tragedy

## Act Now

America needs more Benjamin Strongs today. Now is the time to act out our faith in our moral and ethical convictions and spirituality. Our children should be taught the benefits of true friendships (see Chapter Eleven). Also, they should be taught how to be friendly and how to maintain friendships. School teachers and college or university professors should endeavor to be approachable and friendly persons instead of making the campuses the bee-hives of hostilities and violence.

College and university administrators, in particular, should endeavor to treat all students and teaching faculty as friends. The president of any college or university and the principals of schools should be the friendliest of persons. After all, the society looks up to them as the cream of society and the people involved in the most blessed career -- the nurturing and development of leaders for the society.

William J. Kreidler, a classroom teacher for twenty years in Cambridge, Massachussetts, incorporates the principles of friendship in his materials and workshops on conflict resolution. He believes that elementary school teachers can use two especially helpful activities to teach children about making and keeping friends.[22] In the first activity, students are paired up and asked to trace each other's outlines on mural paper. Then they are asked to write down the things friends should not do outside the outline.

For the second activity, students are asked to write

down words which describe friendly and unfriendly behaviors. The students use these words to make up class rap songs. The time it takes for these activities is about thirty minutes. Kreidler provides some guideline questions to aid the class discussions.

Another teacher, Terry Martinez, who has been teaching for twenty-four years and works in Fresh Meadow, New York, tries to build a friendship bridge with special-ed kids at her school. Like Kreidler, she believes that teachers can build an effective relationship between normal students and special education students through disability workshops.

In the workshops, teachers develop integrative activities which help normal students to develop their understanding and friendship with handicapped children. A special Olympics is held at the end of the activities where both the normal and disabled students participate.[23] The efforts of Kreidler and Martinez are highly commendable. Hopefully, other teachers will follow their example.

## Some Practical Suggestions

1.    College and university admissions officers should vigorously scrutinize the autobiographical essays that students submit (prior to acceptance) and required by many institutions. Those essays could reveal the goal of a prospective student. They could also tell the cultural and social backgrounds of the students. Perhaps, it may be possible to glean from such essays what motivates a particular student to want to study at a particular college. Should this essay writing not be required from all incoming freshmen?

2. Administrators and heads of departments should be particularly sensitive and friendly toward foreign students. The Orientation Day(s) programs should be made with some friendship principles and strategies in mind. It must be remembered that, as our world becomes smaller and smaller through modern communication technology, many of the people who choose a college and graduate from it become the ambassadors of it. The impression a school or university officer makes upon a foreign student can leave an indelible mark upon him or her.[24]

I shall never forget how I felt on the day that I arrived at Malone College in 1980. The Admissions Officer and my host family were at the airport to welcome me. One may say that this is possible only in a small college. But I also had a warm welcome at Ashland College, a larger college, when I was admitted there. I was very well received at Baylor University, a university with as many or more students as Howard University. I have very fond memories of Baylor.

In contrast, when in 1984, I went to Howard University in Washington, D. C. for the Ph.D. program, not only was there no welcoming on the day of arrival, but I was treated with incredible inhospitality. I had been admitted into Temple University for a doctoral degree before then. However, I chose to accept the offer from Howard, partly because of the full tuition scholarship I had been offered there and, partly, because it was a college that I could relate to because of my race.

The day I appeared before the admissions office, a light-headed African-American woman challenged my academic credentials and disallowed my registration. Even though I had the papers to show that I was a doctoral student duly admitted with a full tuition scholarship and graduate assistanceship, and I had the Master's degree, too, this woman brushed everything aside and adamantly demanded that I must produce my *high school grades* from Nigeria!

She refused to listen to anything else I had to say. She even sarcastically said that if I flunked during the tenure of my stay there, I should never reappear at her office. She was implying that I was not qualified. It was very demeaning. I was totally bewildered and began to regret coming to Howard. This event was only a foreshadow of the things I would experience at Howard.

Certainly, this officer apparently had no idea what qualified someone to be a doctoral student in the American university. She obviously misrepresented the image of the university. I was finally able to register because of the intervention of the graduate director from the history department. And I did eventually receive a Ph.D. from Howard University.

3. Excursion trips and exchange student programs can offer excellent opportunities for the building of friendships. Those who plan these trips and programs must remember that friendships can be rewarding both to foreign students as individuals and to the university. Who knows, someone may return to be an important financial donor to the institution.

4. The International Student offices at the colleges should be the hub for the building of international relationships. At Howard, I always enjoyed my trips to that office. Baylor University's international office programs were probably some of the best anyone could find in America. The special days for international students were unforgettable. And the late Ms. Vernice

Robinson will probably remain the most wonderful person that worked for Baylor in that office.

Malone College in Canton, Ohio, had an unforgetable event for its few internationals when I was there in 1980-1981. Its president and faculty were approachable and friendly. Foreign students went on excursion trips with some faculty and had fun during the trips. The college appeared to respect the cultures of the different internationals by encouraging dialogue and mutual understanding. We even had group photographs!

It is my hope that those persons at the institutions of learning in America who read this chapter will benefit from these suggestions. Friendships made at the school, college, or university level can turn out to become the most indispensable and rewarding experiences in our lives.

## CHAPTER TEN

# FRIENDSHIP
# ACROSS RACIAL LINES

*Show me a true friend of the human race and I'll show you a man who has many friends across racial lines.*

— E. S. Etuk

*The problem of the twentieth century is the problem of the color line.*

— W. E. B. DuBois

One day I was in a restroom at one of the large state-run universities in the U. S. And there, before me, on the wall, was this bold inscription: *"I am not a racist. I just hate everybody."* Quickly, many things ran through my mind, such as, "oh God, let me not run into this kind of creature." "What kind of students is this university producing?" Then, reflectively, I asked myself: "What kind of spiritual and social backgrounds does this student have?" I found myself wondering out loud, unaware that I was speaking to myself in a restroom: "Oh, what kind of friends can this type of writer keep?"

If you think carefully about the restroom citation quoted above, its author is right about one point. You don't have to be a racist to hate everybody. But, you certainly cannot be hating everyone and keeping many good and long-lasting friends. If you are a racist, you are obviously limited in your number of friends. Certain persons of certain racial groups are automatically excluded from your world of friendships simply and solely because of their race.

W.E.B. DuBois, the great African-American sociologist and philosopher, observed in 1903 that "the problem of the twentieth century is the problem of the color line." More than ninety-five years since DuBois made that prophetic statement, the problems of racism and of race relations in America (and indeed in the world) have not been solved. Recent events in the United States have raised the matter of race and racism to the forefront of public debate and discourse.[2]

One event which has highlighted this discourse was reported in a full-page advertisement in the *Philadelphia News* on September 12, 1996. The advertisement was for "The Burned Churches Fund." It stated that since January 1995, seventy-six African-American church buildings in the United States had been burned or desecrated. In the month of August 1995 alone, nine churches were torched and burned to the ground. *Charisma* magazine in August 1997 revealed that of the 81 suspects involved in these church burnings, 55 were white people. It said: "About 160 of 199 persons arrested for the crimes were white, 34 were black and five were Hispanic." The advertisement further stated, "We must fight the fires." But the great question is --"how?"

First, I do not pretend to have all the answers and solutions to the problems of race and racism. That kind of discussion lies beyond the scope of this chapter. But I strongly believe that we must be clear about what race and racism are, and what they are not, if we intend to make friends beyond our own racial groups. We should understand that there is nothing wrong with the idea of a proper identification with one's race. Having said this, I must add that there are a lot of things wrong with racism.

In order for us to build strong friendships across racial lines, we must be very clear about race, racism and the roles that these play in friendship relationships. So, let us begin with the first and primary question: "What is race?" before we attempt to define what is racism. Thereafter we can consider how to build a friendship with someone of a different race. We should bear in mind that too often our attitudes toward people of another race are based upon what Professor Joseph E. Harris called "a tradition of myths and stereotypes." Our attitudes are often rooted in our prejudices and unfounded fears.

### The Meaning of Race

Very few people, including scholars, have successfully defined the term "race." There appears to be two schools of thought about race: those who believe that race is important and those who think that there is nothing like race or that its significance has diminished.

The first school of thought includes writers like Thomas F. Gossett whose book, *Race: The History of an Idea in America* appeared in 1963. Gossett analyzed the early race theories of the seventeenth century and ended his book with "the battle against prejudice." This battle was best expressed by the Civil Rights Movement of the 1960s.

Similar members of this school of thought are Winthrop D. Jordan, Joseph R. Washington, Jr., and George M. Frederickson.[3] Some recent authors have emphasized the permanence of race and racism. These include Derrick A. Bell, Andrew Hacker, Janet E. Helms, and Ivan Hannaford,[4] whose book title is similar to that of Gossett's.

Nearly all these writers have no definition of race. They suppose that we know what race is. They simply delve into their discussions. Gossett points out that around 1684, it was believed that there were "four general classifications of what would now be called races."[5] By the nineteenth century, the efforts in classification wound up with two groups-- the monogenesists (those who believe all humans originated from one source) and the polygenesists (those who believe that all humans originated from more than one source).

Neither George Frederickson nor any of the authors mentioned herein have adequately defined what race is. The historian Ronald Sanders reminds us that the problem with the definition of race is connected with the history of the development of the idea. He writes that "the idea of race was...only a dim and sporadic one to most Europeans during the Middle Ages; its outlines did not begin growing distinct until the fourteenth and fifteenth centuries. "[6]

In other words, our ideas about race are very recent, coming to the front during the years of the pioneers of racial ideologies. Those pioneers included Arthur de

Gobineau (1816-1882), the Frenchman generally considered the Father of Racism, Louis Agassiz (1807-1873), Houston S. Chamberlain (1855-1927), Madison Grant (1865-1937) and Josiah C. Nott (1804-1873) of Mobile, Alabama.

The second school of thought about race -- those who believe that race is insignificant or that there is no such thing like race -- include the widely known scholar Ashley Montagu whose book, *Man's Most Dangerous Myth: The Fallacy of Race* first appeared in 1952. As the title of his book suggests, Dr. Montagu considered the idea of race a myth and fallacious.

William Julius Wilson, a professor of Urban Sociology, assumed that since "younger educated black males have finally approached income parity with younger educated white males, "[7] the issues affecting blacks would be more and more centered around the economics of survival and less and less around race and racism. Public policies would be directed toward the economic area rather than race relations. The burning of seventy-six African-American churches has shown how wrong Wilson was.

Seventeen years after Wilson's book first appeared in 1978, Dinesh D'Souza wrote another controversial book, *The End of Racism: Principles For A Multiracial Society* which, by its title, suggests that racism is on its way out. This book has already generated heated debate. Another author, David Theo Goldberg flatly accuses D'Souza of writing "a dangerous book."[8]

The optimism of those who think that racism is disappearing or that race matters are insignificant is shattered by the permanence of racism and racial concerns and conflicts. For, as authors Ali Rattansi and Sallie Westwood have rightly observed, "the spectre that haunts the societies of 'the West' is no longer communism but, both within and outside their frontiers, a series of racisms and ethnonationalisms."[9] The Balkans are smoldering because of these ethnonationalisms.

We find ourselves returning to our initial question, "What is race?" We ought to admit that the meaning depends upon who you may ask. Calvin C. Hernton believes that race is "a biological term ... a scientific construct whereby men may be classified into more or less exclusive groups on the basis of similarities and dissimilarities of physical characteristics."[10]

He maintains that the classification is physical, and only physical. The criteria for this classification are the color of our eyes; color, texture and quantity of hair (including body hair); cranial formation; nasal index; body stance; facial structure; and pigmentation.[11] Based upon this classification, some people believe that there are three main groups of races: the mongoloid, the negroid, and the caucasoid.

I believe that these classifications and groupings are truthfully superficial. For there is no pure race nor pure blood to be found anywhere. People in recorded history have inter-bred, cross-bred, and intermarried. I would challenge anyone to find me a pure-blooded white man or woman anywhere. Who says that when the Moors invaded and occupied parts of Europe centuries ago, there was absolutely no chance of inter-breeding or cross-breeding?

Who says that the blood of many whites does not run in the veins of many Native American Indians during the years of their annihilation in the centuries past? Therefore, we should admit that though it may be hard to properly define race, there are *differences* among the peoples of this world.

The differences I speak of may be due to geographical, cultural, national and language characteristics. Some people are different because of their ideological orientations. And, I really believe that the days for biological or pseudo-scientific rationalization as justification for racism are over. The days for the promotion or exultation of social Darwinism are also gone. Those who hold dearly to these orientations need to re-educate themselves if we are to avert a future race war which Carl Rowan has warned us all could happen.[12]

## What Is Racism?

It's like pornography in the sense that you may not adequately be able to define it. But you know what it is when racism affects you. Most social scientists have no problem defining what racism is. The following are a few examples:

Thomas Sowell writes that "one of the most used and least defined words in the contemporary ideological vocabulary is 'racism'. The most straightforward meaning of racism is a belief in the innate inferiority of some race or races."[13]

George Frederickson states that,

> *Racism is mode of thought that offers a particular explanation for the fact that population groups which can be distinguished by ancestry are likely to differ in culture, status and power. Racists make claim that the such differences are due to immutable genetic factors and not to environmental or historical circumstance.*[14]

D'Souza says that the most "basic definition of racism

remains clear: Racism is an ideology of intellectual or moral superiority based upon the biological characteristics of race." He goes on to add that "racism typically entails a willingness to discriminate based upon a perceived hierarchy of superior and inferior races. "[15]

Joseph Barndt has a five-word definition: "Racism is prejudice plus power."[16] He argues that racism goes beyond prejudice. He also claims that there are many prejudiced people who are not really racists. Many people who read this will agree with him. And Clyde W. Ford states that "racism is any action or attitude conscious or unconscious, that subordinates an individual or group based on skin color or race. This subordination can be enacted individually or institutionally. "[17]

A straightforward definition of racism is provided by Hernton:

> *Racism may be defined as all of the learned behavior and learned emotions on the part of a group of people towards another group whose physical characteristics are dissimilar to the former group; behavior and emotions that compel one group to conceive of and to treat the other on the basis of its physical characteristics alone, as if it did not belong to the human race.*[18]

The point to bear in mind here is "learned." It implies, as Hernton has forcefully argued, that racism is learned. No one, not even the head of the Ku Klux Klan, is born a racist. People learn to discriminate, to segregate, to denigrate and to despise those they have learned to disassociate with. People learn to believe that they are better than others.

As I observe my own children, I am convinced that no human child was born a racist. My four year-old son plays with anyone who comes his way: white, black, Oriental, Jewish, American Indian, whatever. He can only learn racism from his parents or choose to become a racist if he so desires when he becomes older.

However, Terry Stull, a Christian minister residing in Rantoul, Illinois calls racism a disease, a very widespread disease in his book, *The Disease of Racism*. According to him, the prevalence of racism is frightening since it affects almost all of us. He stresses that "no race or ethnic group is free from its influence."[19] Anyone who has not been exposed to the crushing blows of racism has no clue as to its dangerous and debilitating effects. Racism is a cancerous, poisonous disease in any society, particularly in the Western society.

## Kinds of Racism

My seminary professor of history once used the term "incipient racism" to describe the popular brand of racism in America today. This means that racism is just beginning to come into being or that it is becoming apparent to many people. But there is nothing "incipient" about racism in the Western world.

Racism has existed ever since the first caucasian came into contact with peoples other than himself. This is the central thesis in Joseph R. Washington, Jr.'s book, *Anti-Blackness In English Religion, 1500-1800* published in 1984. Racism has been part and parcel of the foreign policies of many Western nations. Racism in the Western world went hand in hand with slavery. Now, to deal with racism, we must understand what kinds of racism there are and how each manifests themselves.

Paul Kivel, in his book, *Uprooting Racism: How White People Can Work for Racial Justice* (1996) writes that, "racism is based on the concept of whiteness -- a powerful fiction enforced by power and violence."[20] Here the implication is that racism is a white thing perpetrated only by whites. This view raises the question whether or not non-whites can be racists. Can a black person be a racist? I shall return to this issue later.

But let us consider whiteness as a kind of racism and ask the question, "what is whiteness?" Ruth Frankenberg who dedicated her book, *White Women, Race Matters: The Social Construction of Whiteness* "to those who struggle for a day beyond racism -- to a time when this book will be read as history and not as a study of the present," concluded that "race shapes white women's lives."[21] And, she emphatically maintained that whiteness is "a place from which white people look at ourselves, at others, and at society."[22] If so, then what's wrong with that?

Quite frankly, nothing except insofar as that place of standing to look at 'others' does not imply abuse of power, prejudice, exploitation and oppression. As long as I am not mistreated by the result of one's worldview or perspective, I have nothing against whiteness. Because it would be equally wrong to deny me the right and opportunity to view the world from my African perspective. To borrow the line from author Janet E. Helms, "race is a nice thing to have" as long as it does not harm me or anyone else.

At the conceptual level, social scientist Michael Wieviorka has identified four levels of racism:

♦ Infraracism -- this is the inarticulate stage wherein racism is not a central issue.

- split racism -- this is a level higher than the first. Racism begins to emerge as a central issue. The discourse is articulated.

- political racism- at this stage, racism is at the center of political and intellectual debates.

- total racism- this is the stage at which the state and political machineries are based on racist principles.[23]

Andrew Hacker in *Two Nations: Black and White, Separate, Hostile, Unequal* (1995) asserts that racism expresses itself in three distinct but related ways and adds that racism "rests largely on ignorance... Still, racism is not always based on ignorance."[24] The experts on racial matters would agree with Hacker -- that much of our racial problems are due to gross ignorance on the part of the racist. And these experts have identified the following *eight* kinds of racism:

1. **Biological Racism** -- this is racism founded upon genetic suppositions. Here, pseudo-scientific reasons are offered for the supposed inferiority of another race or races. D'Souza explains that "scientific racism developed out of a major European project in the eighteenth and nineteenth centuries to explore, map, classify, and understand the natural world." But he also adds that,

> *The problem faced by Western scientists and naturalists was a genuine one. In the eighteenth and nineteenth centuries, it was axiomatic in Europe and the United States that apart from enclaves of civilization, the majority of the population in the nonwhite world was plunged in barbarism*[25]

Now I cannot restrain myself but respond by stating that D'Souza's views here expose him to the charge of prejudice. First, what made Europe's problem "genuine" and in whose interest was the solution of their "genuine" problem? What does D'Souza mean by "enclaves of civilization?" He does not state the role of militarism in the development of white civilization and how that militarism was applied to nonwhite peoples and their destinies. Hence, D'Souza tends to support the old school of thought of Eurocentrism. This is, perhaps, one reason his book is perceived as dangerous.

2. **Ideological Racism** -- this is racism rooted in ideology, for example, manifest destiny. In brief, this ideology, like Frederick Lugard's, held that non-white lands and territories, together with their mineral, natural, and human resources, were for the exclusive benefit and enjoyment of the caucasian people. The "native" peoples were to be civilized in order to be Christianized. It did not matter if slavery and colonialism were used in the civilizing process.

3. **Institutional Racism** -- this is racism practiced and bolstered by society's institutions such as the family, schools and colleges, the military, the financial establishments, the churches, the courts, and such racism enforced by laws and the government. Only the most ignorant person unschooled in American history would deny that there has been institutional racism in the United States. Before 1960, it would have been difficult or even unthinkable for a black man or woman to challenge any form of institutional racism in Mississippi or Alabama. Or have we forgotten about George Wallace? Institutional racism in America promoted segregation,

discrimination, exclusion of blacks and other minorities from some social benefits; and in some places, this brand of racism was deemed proper or part of the American way of life. When the Civil Rights activists emerged in the 1960s, they were opposed and, sometimes, murdered because they threatened the status quo. As Joseph Barndt had argued successfully, today's institutional racism is practiced indirectly by subtle and sophisticated means.[26] Clyde Ford does a good job in highlighting how this racism continues today.[27]

4. **Individual Racism** -- this is racism learned, acquired, and practiced by an individual. This is racism by choice and it is often intentional. Anyone can decide to become a racist for various reasons -- nationalism, nativism, economics and even neurosis. Clyde Ford points out that "racism actually begins with people who are unable to accept themselves."[28]

In this instance, the problem might be due to psychological dysfunctionality. But, it should be remembered that a racist can always repent, receive forgiveness, and experience love for those he or she had hated. Terry Stull's analysis of racism is based upon individual responsibility for ending racism in the United States.[29]

In his discussion of individual racism, Barndt reminds us that "racists are made, not born."[30] He adds that "individual racists are created by the systematic empowerment and perpetuation of our personal prejudices."[31] All through their lives, most white people have been isolated, anesthetized, privileged, and conditioned through the process of an education which teaches them that they are physically and mentally superior to any other people.

The irony is that most white people, in spite of this mental conditioning, still fear the black man, particularly the educated, articulate, black man. Why? Because of the fear of matching an able competitor in the open marketplace of life. It is all economic. This is why black leaders in the United States are often emasculated, routinely hounded and even eliminated. Individual fear is at the root of individual racism. J. Edgar Hoover, the former FBI director, best represents this kind of racism. Freedom from racism comes as one takes responsibility for one's own racism. Denial is the ultimate lie.

5. **White Racism** -- this is akin to whiteness; it is racism borne out of whiteness. It is the white group distortion of opinions about people of other races and their ability to enforce such distorted opinions by the misuse of power. Understood in this sense, racism is a white-man's problem. It should be clear that here I am talking about the collective abuse of power by white people. There are, as we have seen, differences between individual racism and the collective form of racism.

6. **Black Racism** -- this is racism that is a counterpart to whiteness; it is racism that flows out of a black mental construct which sees the world from the totality of blackness. Now in the American sphere, it is almost idiotic or even stupid to say that a black person can be a racist. But haven't you heard of a black brother accusing another of not being truly black? And what does being truly black mean? Haven't you heard of the pursuit of black theology and the invention of the black Christ in efforts to replace the white Christ and white theology?

Back in 1972, Moyibi Amoda in *Black Politics and Black Vision* forcefully argued that "a black man is racist in the same sense that a white man is racist, i.e., in the logic of his belief system. But while white racism obstructs the black man's evolution, the black man's racism corrupts the black man from within."

Amoda added: "What is more, since black racism is a response to white racism, the black racist becomes defined in terms of the counter ideal. Just as the white man is defined in terms of blackness, since white is what black is not, in the same way the black racist becomes defined in terms of what white is not. This is the greatest danger of all for the black man."[32]

Amoda observed and complained that there was a perspective within the black movement that can be characterized as racist and that perspective, though functionally beneficial in defining the boundaries of the black ethnic group, "is nevertheless dangerous to the black man in terms of the quality of life which the black nation is to present."[33] A concrete example of what can emerge from the perspective which Amoda complained of is doing theology by coloration.

At Ashland seminary, I analyzed this theology in a paper which I titled "The Theology of Niggerology." I totally endorse the view of Amoda. We cannot let white people's racism turn us into black racists. Martin Luther King, Jr. did not succumb to such an abberation in his theological orientation. This is what gave his message to America its unique beauty and universal acceptance.

7.    **Cultural Racism** -- this is racism which presupposes that one's culture is superior to that of another race. The cultural racist tries to enforce his culture upon another race without finding anything good or decent in that other culture. Generally, white people

have been cultural imperialists.

Many of them went to Africa believing that the African mind was *tabula rasa* and, therefore, there was nothing in the African culture which the whites could appreciate. This is why I am offended when D'Souza speaks of barbarism in the nonwhite world. He has forgotten about cannibals in seventeenth century Virginia and the recent case of a white cannibal in Ohio!

Cultural racists have produced men and women in Africa with a colonial mentality -- who find nothing good in the African way of life. For example, some African leaders would rather drink imported champagne than palm wine. Many white missionaries see all our cultural artifacts and relics as idols whereas the museums of many Western cities are filled with the same "idols" stolen out of Africa. Cultural racism is responsible for this mess.

8. **Sexualized Racism** -- this is the most hypocritical aspect of racism; it is racism based upon the "purity" of the white woman. Until recent times, the white woman was held out to the world as the epitome of purity, untouchable by the inferior races, chaste and adorable, and any sort of contamination through sexual intercourse with a non-white deserved the lynching of such a non-white.

On the one hand, blacks were not to touch the white woman. But, the white man, by force and abuse of power, reserved to himself the right to have sexual intercourse with the black woman slave or freed. While the white man saw blacks as depraved, barbaric, and savage, these same whites saw nothing wrong in copulating with black women. Thomas Jefferson is a typical example.

Today, one hears so much about the immoral depravity and condition of the black underclass family but many white people in America have short memories. They seem to forget that in some American states slave-breeding was deemed normal and economically beneficial. They forget that many of the founding fathers had slave women with whom they had sex.

They forget how many white women on the plantations seduced and forced their slave men to have sexual intercourse with them. And yet, in the 1990's, it is still a taboo in the white conservative mind for a black man to be seen with a white woman, let alone marrying a white woman. After careful consideration, it is my contention that, beyond economics, sex is at the root of American racism.

The lynching of many blacks is still possible and continues today in many refined ways because of a black man's relations with a white woman. So long as the white vagina is purer than silver and is considered untouchable, so long shall racism persist in the United States of America. And, as long as the black man's rage in this matter is not assuaged, so long shall violence and brutal murders continue. The sad thing about this sexualized racism is that much of the violence is black on black crime.

Author Calvin C. Hernton points out that highest in the scale of thinking of many whites is their fear that most blacks want to intermarry and have sex with white women. However, Gunnar Myrdal found out in 1944 that the highest concern of black men was not sex with white women but having economic opportunities for their progress. So, we see how different and far apart the two worlds are. Hernton maintains that the sexualization of racism is a reality.

I have written elsewhere how, in Ohio, during my seminary years, a white woman in the library, in broad daylight, nearly screamed because I walked behind her in search of books for my term papers. I was very embarrassed. Many white women have caused the death of an innocent black man because they have been conditioned to believe that the average black man wants to rape a white woman. But who screams when a black sister is raped by a white man?

This sexualization of racism is a serious matter if we are to make friends outside our own racial groups. Someone must clean up his or her misconceptions first or no true and meaningful friendship can occur. If you want to test how serious a white man is about racial reconciliation and equality, ask him if he would ungrudgingly give out the hand of his daughter in marriage to an able and suitable black bachelor, without any regrets?

Thus far, I have attempted to show what race and racism are and I have highlighted the kinds of racism that one may confront. I do not consider it necessary to rehearse all the destructive consequences of racism. Many books are replete with that information. Just for emphasis, let me cite Andrew Hacker who says that, "If we care about racism, it is because it scars peoples lives.... The significance of racism lies in the way it consigns certain human beings to the margins of society, if not to painful lives and early deaths."[34] Racism is destructive. We know this fact to be true. It is America's national killer, as the recent racial murder in Jasper, Texas, has shown.

What we need is a willingness and a readiness to confront the hinderances to anti-racism: ignorance, fear, myth of the purity of the white female, fear of ostracism, and downright stupidity. We need to come to grips, as the anti-apartheid South African activists did, with the fact that racism is a sin against God and against humanity.

Personally, I do not believe that this world is moving toward a non-racial society. I do not believe that racism can or will be completely eradicated in the United States and in this world. That is sheer naivete and the delusion of the liberals.[35] I believe that racism is a disease afflicting the human soul, mind, body, and spirit. Legal enactments and education may help to a degree but can never take away the sin of racism. The Christian gospel has the power to cure any racist.

I do share the idealism of Martin Luther King, Jr. who looked forward to a time when we shall be judged, not by the color of our skin, but by the content of our character. It is a noble ideal. And, that's all it is. But we must bear in mind that white America never allows you to forget about your color. It is endemic with whites to be color-conscious and colorbiased.

I lived for over 30 years without fully understanding what racism was. In my village, people are not perceived in terms of color. Identity is based on the family line, village location, clan and nationality. But when I arrived in the United States in 1980, suddenly, I became "a nigger," a black man, "colored," a minority, terms not used before to describe who I am.

I knew white people as Americans, Englishmen, Irishmen, Europeans, Frenchmen, Germans, Russians and so forth. But, in the course of nearly two decades, I have unconsciously imbibed the racial vocabulary in America. That is sad. Those who deny the persistence or permanence of racism are part of the problem in finding lasting solutions to our racial conflicts.

## Building Friendship Across Racial Lines.

The central task of this chapter was to explore ways of building friendship across racial lines. But we had to traverse a difficult terrain before completing our task. Now, we must state some of those ways by which we can build inter-racial friendships. These include:

♦ Gaining knowledge of the history and culture of people different from our own. Every white person should take a class in African and African-American history or Japanese history or Chinese history. Americans are terribly ignorant about the histories of other peoples.

♦ Appreciating the cultures and values of other people. I knew nothing of pumpkin pie (my favorite dish) before coming to America. In my village, we do not eat pumpkin this way. But I now love pumpkin pies. I have a strong love for and appreciation of American democracy and freedom. That does not mean that the life I lived prior to coming to America was barbaric or primitive. In fact, I cherish my village upbringing. That life was simply different.

♦ Opening up our lives and homes to be enriched by other influences and peoples. Some of my white American friendships are the most wonderful things that have happened to me. I have gained wider knowledge of the world around white people. This openness is unavoidable.
I do not understand some of my black brothers and sisters who speak the white man's language, use forks and knives manufactured by whites, fly the aeroplanes

designed and manufactured by whites, use the currency manufactured and controlled by whites, attend colleges and universities where white philosophies and technologies are taught, and then turn around to repudiate all things white. Some brothers can't even manufacture a spoon! This is craziness. We must open up to our vulnerability. This is being human. But we have God to trust and He can be our guide in racial matters as in every other matter.

♦ Living out the true Christian life of loving our neighbors. "Who is my neighbor?" is an age-old question. But Jesus Christ did not leave us in doubt. Racists, discriminators, and segregationists cannot truly say that they love their neighbors in a Christian context. White people who push blacks out of their churches through all kinds of subtle means and manipulations cannot be true ambassadors of Jesus Christ.

♦ Asking God for the spirit of humility to repent from the sin of racism. I am glad to observe that many efforts are already geared in this direction. Not too long ago, a major American denomination called for racial reconciliation and repentance for the racial sins of the past. The Promise Keepers, Inc. is also very much in earnest, working for racial reconciliation in the body of Christ. We cannot say how sincere and genuine these efforts are. But, time will tell.

♦ Encouraging interracial marriages where they are motivated by genuine love and mutual respect. The evidence that I have indicates that interracial marriages in America are increasing. This trend should not alarm our white brothers. Instead, we should know that love is color-blind and, certainly, heaven will be color-blind.

*Love in Black and White: the Triumph of Love Over Prejudice and Taboo* (1992) is the story of Mark Mathabane, a Kaffir boy from South Africa who left his country in 1978 at the age of eighteen on a tennis scholarship to study. (See Chapter One where I first mentioned his name). Mark fell in love with Gail, a white American girl raised in the all-white communities of Ohio and Texas. The two never dreamed of marrying outside their races. But they fell in love and married.

Mark and Gail now live in Kernersville, North Carolina, with their two children, Bianca and Nathan. *Publishers Weekly* said that theirs is "a stirring interracial love story," while the *Library Journal* called it "a hymn of praise."[36] Readers of this book will discover that it takes courage and risk to combat racism and to uphold the common brotherhood and sisterhood of the human family.

In racial matters, I am an optimist only in the sense that my Christian training reinforces my faith in a sovereign God who "hath made of one blood all nations of men to dwell on all the face of the earth" (Acts 17:26). Friendship across racial lines is possible if we ask God to help us love everyone just as He does and as Jesus Christ, His son, did.

The title of Clyde W. Ford's book, *We Can All Get Along: 50 Steps You Can Take To Help End Racism* (1994), suggests that I am not alone in my optimism. There are many people who would like to see the end of this terrible social monster called racism. But we must first overcome our fears, our apathies, and our reluctance to do something about it. We must refuse to deny the existence of racism. Rather, we must get all the information we need and act quickly to stop racism.

We must never forget that every racist action is, indeed, a violation of the freedom and human rights of someone who God has created and embraced as a member of the human family. If every reader of this chapter would determine to establish a friendship relationship with someone of another race in the course of the next year, I would have achieved my aim.

# CHAPTER ELEVEN

## THE BENEFITS OF FRIENDSHIP

*Nothing in the world is more excellent than friendship... It's like taking the sun out of the world to bereave human life of friendship .*

— Cicero

We live in a very materialistic and utilitarian world, one in which a person is prone to ask the question "what's in it for me?" regarding almost every important matter or idea. I would not be surprised if someone would ask me: "what's the big deal about friends and friendships?" What are the benefits of friendship?

This chapter examines twelve benefits of friendship. It attempts to provide a reasoned discourse and answer to your question. It is my hope that the twelve benefits presented here will challenge and inspire you to invest the time necessary to develop quality friendships. First, I would like to look at what some great historical figures said about the value of friendship. Thereafter, I will present the twelve benefits. Let's begin with Aristotle.

**Aristotle** (384-322 B.C.), one of the great philosophers of the Western world, wrote that "the ancients listed friendship among the highest virtues ... For without friends, no one would choose to live, though he had all other goods."[1] "In poverty and other misfortunes of life, he added, "true friends are a sure refuge. The young they keep out of mischief; to the old they are a comfort and aid in their weakness, and those in the prime of life they incite to noble deeds."[2]

**Plato** (428-348 B.C.), a giant in the rank of Aristotle and a believer in the supremacy of ideas, said that a "true friendship between man and man is infinite and immortal."[3] **Euripides** (485 -406 B.C.) held that "Life has no blessing like a prudent friend."[4] For **Joseph Addison** (1672 -1719 ), the value of friends lay in the fact that "friendship improves happiness and abates misery, by doubling our joy, and dividing our grief."[5]

**Francis Bacon** (1561-1626) believed that "those friends are weak and worthless, that will not use the privilege of friendship in admonishing their friends with freedom and confidence, as well of their errors as of their danger."[6] He added that "it is a mere and miserable solitude to want true friends, without which the world is but a wilderness."[7] Furthermore, Bacon contended that "no receipt openeth the heart but a true friend, to whom you may impart griefs, joys, fears, hopes, suspicions, counsels, and whatsoever lieth upon the heart to oppress it, in a kind of civil shift or confession."[8]

For **Cicero**, "nothing in the world is more excellent than friendship ... It's like taking the sun out of the world to bereave human life of friendship."[9] It is in this light that **James Boswell**, the Scottish lawyer and biographer of Samuel Johnson, called friendship "the wine of life."[10] One lightens and gives warmth and life to the universe and the other gladdens the heart of man. Friendship is here compared to the sun and wine.

**Samuel Johnson** stated that "the greatest benefit which one friend can confer upon another, is to guard, and excite, and elevate his virtues."[11] **Socrates** (469-399 B.C. ), ranked in importance with Plato and Aristotle, admonished: "Oblige with all your soul that friend who has made you a present of his own."[12] An Italian proverb contends that he "who finds himself without friends is like a body without a soul."[13]

**William Alger** wrote that "A pure friendship inspires, cleanses, expands, and strengthens the soul."[14] According to the Chilean poet, **Pablo Neruda** (1904-1973 ), "friendships strengthen the bond of brotherhood for all of humanity."[15] An anonymous poet likens new friends to silver, the old friends to gold; and he advises us to make new friends but to also keep the old friends.

**Saint John Chrysostom** (345-407 A.D. ) observed that "a faithful friend is the medicine of life; for what cannot be effected by means of a true friend? or what utility, what security, does he not afford? What pleasure has friendship? The mere beholding him diffuses an unspeakable joy, and at the bare memory of him the mind is elevated."[16] With this lofty sense of friendship in mind, **William Shakespeare** said that when he thought of the "precious" friends he possessed, he would gladly have scorned to change his state with kings.[17]

In 1841, **Ralph Waldo Emerson** wrote that friendships were gifts and expressions of God. He explained that such relationships were formed "when the divine spirit in one individual finds the divine spirit in another."[18] Elsewhere, he stated that "God evidently does not intend us all to be rich, or powerful, or great, but he does intend us all to be friends."[19] Here the emphasis is on "us all" and this is very inclusive.

Emerson's contemporary was **Henry David Thoreau**. Thoreau advised: "Think of the importance of friendship in the education of men. It will make a man honest; it will make him a hero; it will make him a saint. It is the state of the just dealing with the just; the magnanimous with the magnanimous, the sincere with the sincere; man with man."[20]

Thus, by the utterances of these fifteen historical figures we are informed that "friendship is a deep thing. It is, indeed, a form of love,"[21] as William Bennett has contended recently. The voices of these historical giants clearly and eloquently declare that friendships are vital and are of inestimable value. The wonder of it all is that few people take the time to consider the value of friendships, much less take the time to develop and deepen their friendship relationships. They act as if this is unimportant until there is a crisis!

We should never forget that Napoleon died miserably and friendless because, as he himself once put it, "I made courtiers; I never pretended to make friends."[22] Someone should have passed on to him the insightful advice of Emerson who said that "the only way to have a friend is to be one."[23] "On a rocky little island", Bruce Barton wrote, "[Napoleon] fretted away the last years of his life - alone."[24]

I really wonder how many of us reading this would want to end up like Napoleon when our last sunset and evening light ebbs away. So, what are some of the other benefits that friendships can offer? Consider the following:

### 1. A Great Support System

For fifty years, Thomas Jefferson had a near-perfect and permanent friendship with James Madison. Nearing his death, Jefferson wrote to Madison regarding their friendship. He referred to the value he had derived from this relationship as a "pillar of support through life."[25] How many of us do dread the thought of dying alone, with no friends around to cheer us on to that country which no traveler returns?

We can agree with Jefferson that friendship does provide a vital support system in everyday life. I recall when my wife and I had our first child. We desperately needed help as she was about to deliver our baby. I then realized the awesome necessity of good friends. Like an old friend, Mabel Cruz, a pastor's wife, came to our rescue to help us with some service and support. When our son was born five years later, we had Maria who arrived on time to transport us to the hospital that night.

### 2. Antidote For Loneliness

In our real world, it is impractical to be a hermit. The hermit is one prone to the world of loneliness. It is friendship which supplies us with the kind of people who may rescue us from loneliness. It is important to bear in mind the clear admonition of Emerson: "the only way to have a friend is to be one." I wonder if the unabomber, Theodore J. Kaczynski, had a real friend, even in his family. I doubt if he had much of a support system. If he did, how then did he become a hermit who ended up murdering innocent people?

Judith Viorst writes that "in addition to helping us

grow and giving us pleasure and providing aid and comfort, our intimate friends shelter us from loneliness."[26] In my life which has already spanned half a century, I have not yet met someone who claims that he or she has never been lonely or that he or she is so happy and thrilled with loneliness. But I have met with many people who have shared with me their desperate need for intimate friendships. One man said to me: "Nobody cares for me and when I die, no one will care." It was sad, very sad, to hear this.

### 3. Personal Uplift

Good friends bring you up, that is to say, they can incite us to the higher purposes of life. They can spur us to personal growth - be such growth moral, intellectual, spiritual, and even economic. I am reminded of my friend Charles whom I first met at Baylor University's graduate school in Waco, Texas. I came to know Charles as a hard-working, meticulous, and ambitious African student. Charles spurred me to do my very best at Baylor. Today, we both have Ph.D.'s

Recently, Charles was instrumental in helping me find a teaching position at one of the colleges in Maryland. We have been friends for over sixteen years. I spent a night at his home recently that enabled us to reminisce about our time at Baylor. Friendship with Charles has had a very positive impact on my intellectual growth. Concerning this, Viorst writes that "in adolescent friendships we use our friends, as we use our lovers, to discover, confirm and consolidate what we are."[27] This kind of friendship enhances our self-esteem and allows us to be the best with ourselves.

Indeed, this kind of friendship can help broaden our

horizons.     Not  long  ago,  Charles  unexpectedly
announced that he was about to graduate from a law
school in 1998.  He had been teaching political science for
sometime and had quietly been studying law.  I saw this
as a broadening of the field or horizon for him and, thus,
was challenged and inspired to advance to a higher level
myself.  I am a historian, but also believe that if I end up
tomorrow as a lawyer, it will be because of Charles and
the inspiration he offers.  It is a good thing to have such a
friend who lifts me up by his accomplishments.

### 4. Ally

A real friend is the best ally one can find anywhere and
have at any time.  Who else can better qualify than the
one to whom we may unburden our hearts?  Such an ally
may not betray us.  They are our comrades.  They
provide the "stand-by-me loyalty" which William Bennett
writes of in his book, *The Book of Virtues*.  They can go to
great lengths to perform acts of sacrifice, even unto death,
on our behalf.

In this respect, Bennett introduces us to the great,
heroic, story of Damon and Pythias during the fourth
century B.C. Dionysius, the ruler of Syracuse, one of the
Sicilian city-states, had become annoyed with Pythias on
account of his denunciation of the ruler's tyranny and
absolutism. Dionysius had asked Pythias to retract but he
refused.  So Pythias was imprisoned and sentenced to
death.

When asked to make a last wish before his death,
Pythias requested that he be allowed to visit his wife and
children, to say goodbye. He pledged to return to face his
execution. Dionysius was not  persuaded that he would
return. And, before Pythias could say another word,

Damon his friend, volunteered to be remanded in prison until Pythias returned. Damon almost lost his life because Pythias was late in coming back. Damon was willing to give up his own life for his friend. Dionysius was moved by this act of love and reversed his sentence because of it.[28]

This story reveals to what extent a true ally may go to defend us as friends. How many such allies do we have today? The story of Damon and Pythias also reminds me of the fate of the twelve allies of Jesus Christ. They were the best examples of true friendship and love. Although their master had been crucified by the Roman authorities for a treasonable felony, the disciples readily risked their lives in the defense of the cause of their master and friend.

It is important for each of us to know that somebody, other than ourselves, cares so much for us; that we are preciously prized and that we matter. This kind of knowing responds to our deeper human need related to our worth. The actions of our allies may be inexplicable. Yet, our longing need remains undeniable. Friendship satisfies this need and is a benefit to the recipient. Friendship in this case becomes the basis for the display of our acts of courage and ultimate sacrifice.

### 5. Assistance

It is nearly axiomatic that every true friendship involves mutual assistance between the parties connected. Friends can be real helpers. A popular Nigerian saying is that a friend in need is a friend indeed. What would our world be like if we had no such friends whose friendships become the vehicles for sharing, for help to one another, for openness, for support in our moments of vulnerability, and for standing by us in our joys and in our adversities?

Our lives would be much worse without them. Helping friends does cheer the faint and weary; make the timid spirit brave; warn the erring; lighten the dreary pathway. They also nurture, strengthen, widen, and lengthen man's relationship with man.[29]

## 6. Proper Childhood Development

Friendship is vital to the proper development of children. Bennett reminds us that every parent knows how crucial the choice of friends is for every child. "Childhood friendships", he insists, "tell parents which ways their children are tending. They are important because good friends bring you up, and bad friends bring you down."[30] As the old saying goes: "Show me your friends and I'll show you your character".

Social psychologists Drs. Carin Rubenstein and Phillip Shaver corroborate this view. They analyzed the role of playmates in early child development and found that friendship is important in their preparation for adult social roles and adult sexuality. They point out that children who are raised without playmates tend to suffer from peer rejections and may be withdrawn from their social groups.

Conversely, childhood friendships provide the ground for teamwork, playmates, and the learning of social rules from their peers. Such children easily grow up with self-assurance and acceptance. They also grow up feeling that they belong to the group and to the community at large.[31] They are well-rounded for life within the community and are not intimidated by peer pressure.

My wife and I were very concerned about the availability of the right kind of playmates and friends for our children when we moved in December 1996. We were moving out of an apartment complex we had occupied for eleven years to a house that we had purchased. We did not know anyone at the neighborhood, and especially, what kinds of kids our children would play with.

We were quite concerned. We began deliberately to open our home to the children from our new neighborhood. Children, being what they are, it was not long before our children adjusted to their new friends and playmates. My wife and I also felt comfortable with the new children. What would life be like for our children without their precious new companions?[32]

The celebrated case of Helen Keller (1880-1968) is also worth mentioning here. Born in Tuscumbia, Alabama, Keller was an American author and lecturer who, though deaf, blind, and mute, inspired millions with her life of achievements. Keller's life was transformed by her friendship with Anne Mansfield Sullivan, an Irish immigrant who became Keller's teacher from the Boston Perkins Institute for the Blind.

It was Sullivan who taught Keller at the age of seven that everything had a name. By 1904, aided and mentored by Sullivan, Keller completed college and set out to write her autobiography, *The Story of My Life*, which became a classic. Whatever Keller became was undoubtedly due to her steadfast and abiding friendship with Anne Sullivan.

Emmanuel Hart, one of my childhood friends, was from Bonny in the Riverian coastlands of Nigeria where much of the crude oil is produced. My reflection now is that we were soulmates. We enjoyed each other's company to such an extent that we were often inseparable. Although Emmanuel was of a different ethnic group, anyone who saw us in those days would have thought that we were of the same ethnic origin because we were so close to each other.

Unfortunately, those were the days in Nigeria when tribalism had not yet cut so deep into the social and political fabric of the country as to render it a dangerous liability to national development. I lost track of Emmanuel during the Nigerian civil war and have greatly missed the real playmate of my childhood years. I wish that I could rediscover him! He was very special to me.

### 7. Catalyst For Love

Exactly when love begins among two individuals no one can really be too sure. But one can be sure that friendship can be a catalyst for love. Perhaps, for mere debate, one may argue that love comes before a friendship. Many social scientists believe that friendship is a good breeding ground and the nurturer of lasting love.

So much of what goes on today in American society is not love. It is simply LUST - raw, crude, yes, libidinous sex. Since the 1960s, liberalism and relativism have allowed youngsters to trivialize love. One only has to sit in front of the Jerry Springer T.V. show and see America at its worst. For one thing, this television show reveals how depraved some Americans have come to imbibe and defend these modern concepts of love and a loving relationship.

In 1990 when I published my book, *A Walk Through the Wilderness,* I had deplored this trivialization of love. Here are some current examples of the notions of love:

♦ Beer drinkers make better lovers," declares a lisenceplate of a car parked on one of the streets in the nation's capital.

♦ "Love is holding hands at the movies, a moonlight sail, mom's apple pie, seeing your name in the sky... sending a love note in the Post classified Valentine section."[33]

♦ Two sisters, in their twenties, are having a lesbian relationship; but one of them is married to a man. The two sisters also have sex constantly with their cousin. On national television one of these sisters argues that since she is so much *in love* with her lesbian sister, her husband must accept her lesbianism if he truly loved her. Crazy indeed!

♦ Another woman is having sex with another woman but insists that her husband keep off from any other woman because doing that would violate the sacredness of their marriage relationship. She claims that she is *in love* with her husband but that she has a right to experiment with another woman.

Today, one can love his cat, dog or snakes more than he loves his mother and not feel guilty about it! In our modern and romantically hedonistic world, love has been trivialized. Love without responsibility is the curse of modern America. "If it feels good, do it" is the popular slogan taught to our youth.

Without offense to anybody, America is fast becoming a country of sexmaniacs and moneymaniacs. In 1991, 54 million Americans confessed that they were "sexually insatiable."[34] There are no more taboos, no restraints, and no shame. Anything goes and sodomy is nearly acceptable. It seems as if nobody understands that true friendship cannot support these faulty and dubious notions of love.

In Chapter Two where we examined the meaning of friendship, we noted that this kind of relationship is intolerant of deceptions, cheating, lies, and selfishness. None of the characters we analyzed would tolerate these elements in their friendship relations. Think again of the descriptions or definitions of friendship by Jeremy Taylor, Plato, Cicero, Montaigne, Solomon, C.S. Lewis, Aristotle, Socrates, Emerson, Thoreau, David, Jonathan, Ruth, and Naomi.

Does any sane person really believe that true friendships do not demand respect and admiration for the noble character? And what of trust and fidelity? Would George Burns and Jack Benny have remained friends for fifty-five years without trust and faithful loyalty? Would their friendship have lasted that long? How can a son and his father benefit from their friendship without commitment, faithfulness, respect, and loyalty? It simply would not work.

How can a daughter respect and trust her mother who is swinging from one man to another man? Would such a mother not be a hypocrite if she were to admonish her daughter to play it safe with the guys? In all these circumstances, it is clear that friendship provides the grounds for love which may lead to marriage. Both friendship and love are very deep things.

Dr. Lillian B. Rubin, the internationally recognized author who studied the role of friendship in our lives, discovered that love and friendship tend to compete for each other in children. As young people grow, romance temporarily wins over friendship. The pull toward love gets stronger until the "new love" looms larger than friendship.

Rubin writes that "it's another of those ironic contradictions that friendship, which gains it's power and force out of our need to separate from the family into which we were born, now becomes the casualty of our search for a new family." She adds: "when this happens, friends are expected to understand and accept that love is a more compelling priority than friendship."[35] She explains: "Friendship, while not unimportant, remains at the periphery of attention rather than at its center."[36]

My understanding of Rubin's explanation here is about the intensity of love in a friendship tangle, not the abolition of friendship. Because, for love to abide and be fruitful, it must be nurtured by genuine friendship. It is best, perhaps, to say that friendship is the precursor to any meaningful love relationship. Those who have jumped into "love at first sight" without friendship often pay a terrible price, including a life of sorrowful or painful regrets.

Like young people dating, it's simply a matter of exercising common sense and parental guidance. In fact, the Christian approach to the love process promotes friendship first before one falls in love. This is because, as C.S. Lewis believed, love is "eminently spiritual, not some exultation of instinct."

The book, *I Loved A Girl* [37] by Walter Trobisch, is based upon this foundation. Popular culture pays little or no attention to the Christian verdict on human relationships. The playboy mentality has in-fused into what is called loving today. America is dying from the lack of friendships prior to love and marriage.

## 8. Life's Enrichment

Now, recall the words by Addison when he said that fiendships improve happiness and abate misery; they double our joys and minimize our griefs. This is clearly part of friendship's benefits. When I consider deeply this matter of life's enrichment, I remember that the Ibibios of Nigeria have a saying: *Owo edi inyene*, meaning, people are riches, or properly put, having people as friends makes one rich.

My uncle Obio-Offiong's wife named her first son (my cousin), *Akaninyene* (meaning: more than riches or greater than riches). And Paul Laurence Dumbar, the African-American poet, described friends as "wealth without measure".[38] Bari-Ellen Roberts, who recently and successfully fought a long civil rights battle with Texaco, admitted that she was truly rich because of her friendships.

Both the Ibibios, all African-Americans, and nearly all people the world over agree that life can be enriched by the possession of good and real friends. The wonderful pieces of advice which friends freely offer, the sharing of their wisdom, the moments of laughter and fun, the feelings of safety and refuge from danger when they are present, the pleasure of their companionship, all these add spice to life. Without these, life would really be empty, "a wilderness," as Francis Bacon had rightly observed.

Recently, Cathy Lechner wrote in the Christian magazine *Charisma* as follows: "s much as I chafe when a friend tries to pull me out of my misery, I realize the *value* of having wonderful friends, and I do have several. These are people who are real with me, not the type of people you often meet at church."[39] I believe that this enrichment of life is what Abraham Maslow would have termed "self-actualization," the fulfilment of what it means to be human and be fully satisfied. Friends do really enrich our lives. Honestly now, who wants to invite an enemy over for a picnic?

## 9. Self-Discovery

The ninth benefit of friendship is its ability to lead us into self-discovery. Dag Hammarskjold said: "The longest journey we make is the journey inward."[40] And, writing on self-discovery as an important key to friendship, Paula Ripple says that "it is in the sometimes pain-filled but always life-giving act of offering friendship to another that we and our friend grow in self-knowledge."[41] "We are involved," she expatiates, "in the task of finding out who we are and what it is God has locked in that treasure that is ourselves. We do this in relationship to others who know the same tension."[42]

Rubin examined this matter of self-discovery and agreed that friends are generally "those who seem to us to call up the best parts of ourselves, even while they also accept our darker side." She wrote that we learn much about ourselves in our relationships with friends. These kinds of friends assist us to like ourselves better; they allow us "to test out" various parts of ourselves, and to affirm some new roles which we may undertake.

Sometimes, we may even choose those friends who mirror our fantasies and reflect the dreams of the self we wish we could be. "By permitting us to see ourselves in the mirror of their affection," Rubin added, "friends help to anchor our self-image, to validate our identity."[43] We can agree with Rubin on this score.

In their book, *The Heart of Friendship*, Muriel James

and Louis M. Savary referred to this self-discovery as the "third self." They wrote: "In each third self the friends are drawn together."[44]    Outwardly, such friends may appear quite differently; but within there is an essential likeness. There is usually a "we-ness" to this kind of friendship.

Benjamin Franklin, one of America's founding fathers, belonged to this kind of friendship club which they called the Junto. It met every Friday night to discuss morals, politics, or philosophy and continued for nearly forty years. How many of us today would not pay something in cash for membership into a similar Junto club?

I must emphasize here that the purpose of self-discovery is the betterment of ourselves. It involves the highest degree of trust and fidelity. That self-discovery which provides the stock-in-trade for gossips and slander becomes destructive and may lead to the end of the relationship. In fact, it could bring about the painful experience of guilt or regrets.

Therefore, the partners in "meta-self," as James and Savary also termed it, must be careful in their choice of friends. They must be aware that this self-discovery process involves risk-taking and vulnerability. Maturity is required and this maturity can lead to further spiritual growth and development.

## 10. Liberation

The self-discovery ingredient in a friendship can lead to another benefit. This is liberation. John had cheated on his wife. But he had kept this a secret for many years. This  secrecy had begun to torment him until he met Tom and became his friend. As  John and Tom grew deeper and deeper in their relationship, John one day unburdened his heart to Tom, knowing that he would not be harshly criticized. This disclosure led to freedom and the lessening of the grip of guilt upon John.

Indeed, so many of us desperately need many Toms in our lives. Pastors and many counselors are witnesses to this freedom and liberation experience by their counselees. After all, that is one reason people seek counseling. In her book, *Friendship As Sacrament*, Carmen L. Caltagirone writes that "when two people meet at a level of deep personal love sustained by intimacy, commitment, affirmation and trust, they do not merge with each other so as to lose their individual identities. Instead, they find themselves and thus find new freedom."

She adds: "Liberation is the experience by which we realize in a deeply personal way that we are loved and accepted just as we are. We are liberated through gracious love."[45] Many of us are loaded with guilt and shame because of our past or secret life. We would do well to benefit from the friendship with loving people ready to help us experience freedom and liberation.

However, we must understand that our friends are not expected to condone or excuse our lifestyle. Gracious love never implies approval or the condoning of one's sins. Rather, it means that we have come to experience the grace of God and are ready to share such grace and love with our friends. Our society is in dire need of these kinds of friends and liberators. And we should open up to such friends.

## 11. Longevity

Longevity is another important potential benefit of friendship that is rarely considered by many. Research has shown that close interpersonal relationships can prolong your life. For many years, people did not consider the fact that interpersonal relationships have a direct positive impact upon physical health.

Long before medical science came to acknowledge the connection, King Solomon had observed that, "A merry heart doeth good like a medicine: but a broken spirit drieth the bones" (Prov. 17:22). He also said that "A merry heart maketh a cheerful countenance; but by sorrow of the heart the spirit is broken" (Prov. 15:13). In other words, Solomon was stating that there is a connection between psychological and physical health. How we feel may be directly linked to our health.

"Relationships Can Keep You Healthy", is the title of Chapter Two of a book by Dr. Barbara Powell, a behavioral psychologist. She writes as follows:

> In a 1974 study conducted by Lisa Berkman, Ph.D., of 7,000 people in Alameda County, California, it was found that those who had extensive social ties had death rates two to three times lower than those who were isolated. And a ten-year University of Michigan study of 2,754 adults in Tecumseh, Michigan, echoed these findings: people with the greatest number of social contacts had one-half to one-fourth the mortality rate of those without supportive networks.[46]

Furthermore, in 1989, psychologist professor Dan P. McAdams stated that a 1976 University of Michigan study revealed that "men who showed a strong desire for warm and close relations with others tended to have fewer physical symptoms of illness and psychological symptoms of anxiety." He added that "men high in intimacy motivation report fewer symptoms of strain and less uncertainty about the future. Women high in intimacy motivation are relatively happy and satisfied with their life roles."[47]

These studies and their results confirmed the contention of Dr. James J. Lynch that "lonely people live significantly shorter lives than the general population."[48]

In 1977, Lynch had published *The Broken Heart*, a book whose central and controversial thesis intended to demonstrate that "the lack of human companionship, the sudden loss of love, and chronic human loneliness are significant contributors to serious disease (including cardiovascular disease) and premature death."[49]

Lynch did not prove, nor did he intend to prove, that everyone in a friendship would be physically fit or well. But his investigation did disclose that "the lack of human companionship or disrupted social relationships may lead to the development of arteriosclerosis and sudden death."[50] Arteriosclerosis is a chronic disease characterized by abnormal thickening and hardening of the arterial walls with resulting loss of elasticity. So the dictionary says.

Lynch concluded that "in a surprising number of cases of *premature* coronary heart disease and *premature* death, interpersonal unhappiness, the lack of love, and human loneliness seem to appear as root causes of the physical problems."[51] Medical science was coming closer to acknowledge what Bible believers had always known.

In many parts of the non-western world, ordinary people believe that friendship is linked to well-being. Recall the Ibibio saying that people are riches. The meaning may be connected not only to having money or material things. It may include non-tangible wealth. I remember that the relatives of dying ones are often expected to be present at such critical moments. Why? Perhaps, it is because their presence may aid the journey of the beloved one into the unknown world of the spirits.

Also, it is, perhaps, because our presence with a beloved relative can reduce the fear of death gripping the departing soul. I long to be by the bedside of my aging father when his time comes to leave this earth. Isn't this a universal longing? So, friendship can aid longevity. It can prolong one's life and of those whom we love.

## 12. Networking

Alan McGinnis writes that "from a financial perspective, our friendships are our most valuable commodity."[52] Every salesman in America believes this to be true. And, you have probably heard of the statement: "It's not what you know but who you know." Believe me, I have personally found this to be true. In my career and the marketing of my books, this proposition seems to hold.

In today's job market, it is not what you know that only counts but it is also *who* you know. Networking is very much in place. Let me provide a personal illustration. First, I hold a Ph.D. in history. I also am the author of four books. I am articulate. I am considered a prolific writer. But all these credentials do not guarantee me a job in the marketplace.

I have to have some colleagues and be able to network with them when I search for a job. It is the reality of the situation. Who are my real networks? They are my friends, of course. The Ph.D. does not guarantee someone a job these days. I know of some Ph.D.s who drive taxicabs at America's airports! Why would anyone in his best mind train in a field and receive the highest degree in that field and then end up driving a cab?

Second, I had always thought that writing a book was the loneliest, most difficult, work. I was wrong. I have found out that publishing your book is the next difficult task. And the most difficult work in the book business is to sell, to market your book. It is even much more difficult if you are black and an African. So, I have found out that my friends constitute my first chain of readers in my book business.

I really do not know how to talk to strangers about my books. I find it easier to talk to my friends first. I have to cherish them in the whole scheme of the networking process. And what would I do without such friends who believe in my message and in what I do? I would be crippled and handicapped. So, networking among my friends has helped me tremendously.

Networking certainly has its financial and other non-monetary rewards. Every book that I write begins with a thought about my friends, who will read the drafts and critically evaluate them before they go out to the editors? Without such friends, I could never be a writer. For, writing is still a very lonely business. But thank God for all my friends.

I have provided the twelve ways in which friendships can benefit us. It is my hope that these benefits will inspire you to wake up and do something about your circle of friends. A life without true, meaningful, friendships is barren, empty, like a wilderness, or like taking the sun out of the world. May God help you to enlarge your circle of friendships.

# CHAPTER TWELVE

## CONCLUSION

*You are my friends.*
            --- Jesus Christ

Bishop Isidore of Seville (560 - 636 A.D.), a seventh-century prolific writer, once said: "When you receive a letter from a friend, dearest son, you should not delay to embrace it as a friend. For it is a fine consolation among the absent that if one is not present, a letter may be embraced instead."[1]

In a way, this book is my letter to you, dear reader, and I want you to embrace it as you would embrace a friend whom you preciously love. I may be absent but I have written to you from the depth of my heart. Through the first eleven chapters of this book, I have sought to impress upon you the utmost importance of friendship.

Everyone needs a friend, as I maintained in the first chapter. But we must understand what we mean by friendship. I sought to clarify the term in the second chapter. There are many loners in America, and, indeed, in the world. This is the thesis of chapter three. But you should not die in loneliness and depression. You can build friendships among men and women, as chapters four and five have shown. I have used the stories of Ruth and Naomi, David and Jonathan, to show that this is possible.

I have contended that friendships are possible and can be made in the home, in the workplace, in the schools, colleges, and universities. They can be made at the churches and across racial lines. In fact, we can have friendships beyond national boundaries. These friendships have many benefits for those engaged in them. You do not lose anything in a friendship. It would be sad if you do not invest time into developing friendships into your life and reap a higher quality of life as a result.

My hope is that you will embrace friendship and cherish it. The quality of friendships that you experience in your life falls under the law of sowing and reaping. The more you sow into relationships, the more you will reap from them. This is a blessing you receive and pass on to others. And, now, I would like to introduce to you my best and most precious friend.

Like Sinedu, this is someone that I have made my king. He is the reason why I live. Without him, life would be utterly hopeless and meaningless for me. Unless he had been my helper, I would have been a total failure. When everybody and all else fails, he alone has remained faithful to me and trustworthy. I love him dearly because of his love for me.

In a few weeks, I will be celebrating my fiftieth birthday. I have lived half a century! I have seen many things, suffered many things, and enjoyed some things. Life has been a school, indeed. There are many mysteries in life, things the intellect and human reasoning alone cannot and will never be able to decipher. But I have found that faith in my friend has seen me through these fifty years. I am persuaded that this constancy of faith will see me through some more years to come.

As it may have been apparent to you, I am a lover of books, for books are the gateway to knowledge. So, let me tell you a story from one of these books that I read recently. This story is about a man whose name you may barely know or remember. But his ministry has touched thousands, if not, millions of lives. This man lived for only forty-six years (1820-1866). His name was Joseph Scriven.[2]

Scriven was born in Dublin. He had been trained as an Anglican pastor. As a young man, he was engaged to be married. On the day before his wedding, his fiancee drowned in a tragic accident. To get away from it all, Scriven left England and emigrated to Canada, heartbroken and almost sick to death.

One day, while a neighbor was keeping him company and consoling him, the neighbor noticed a sheet of paper with some words on it, stuck into Scriven's Bible. He asked to know what it was. Soon this neighbor discovered that it was a song, actually a hymn, which Scriven and a friend had written years before, to comfort his mother during a long illness. He had sought to comfort his mother by sharing some spiritual insights he had gained from the death of his bride-to-be.

Scriven's neighbor was very moved by the words of the song. In time, this song was published and has been used in many Christian churches throughout the world since then. Here are the words of this song:

*What a friend we have in Jesus*
*All our sins and griefs to bear.*

*What a privilege to carry*
*Everything to God in prayer.*
*O what peace we often forfeit*
*O what needless pain we bear*
*All because we do not carry*
*Everything to God in prayer.*

*Have we trials and temptations?*
*Is there trouble anywhere?*
*We should never be discouraged*
*Take it to the Lord in prayer.*
*Can we find a friend so faithful?*
*Who will all our sorrows share?*
*Jesus knows our every weakness*
*Take it to the Lord in prayer.*

*Are we weak and heavy-laden,*
*Cumbered with a load of care?*
*Jesus only is our refuge*
*Take it to the Lord in prayer.*
*Do thy friends despise, forsake thee?*
*Take it to the Lord in prayer*
*In His arms He'll take and shield thee*
*Thou wilt find a solace there.*

Think for a moment about the song of Scriven. It is about my friend Jesus, the Christ. Many people do not care about him. Religious people have made something of an icon about him. Others see him as a very distant figure, transcendent and beyond our human reach. Many others see him as the greatest philosopher, teacher, conqueror, savior, healer and miracle-worker.

Some have merchandised his words for selfish reasons and have profited from his cause. Others dread even to think of him. Yet, still, some hate the very mention of his name, dismissing it as an abstraction, a fiction and a myth. Millions all over the world tend to ignore him. But he is the inescapable Christ.

My precious and best friend is this Jesus. He is the best friend anyone can have. He can help me when I fail. He can keep and hold me lest I fall. I cannot even adequately describe nor explain all of his qualities. In fact, I would not do him justice by even attempting to describe him, for I have never seen him face to face. But I have come to place my faith in him.

For thirty years we have been friends, not in the religious or churchy sense, but in the personal, most intimate way. Through tears and joys, through many sorrows and happy moments, in the silent, darkest night or in the brightest sunny day, particularly, when I am flying some thirty-something thousand feet above sea level, when I am afraid or when I am excited, this very Jesus has been my constant and closest friend.

The wonder of our relationship is that, though I have never seen him, he has made it possible for me to be assured that we are friends. I am not afraid of him. I am in love with him. I really miss him very, very much, especially when I fail to spend quality time with him in prayer. Many times, when I feel strongly for him, my heart pulsates and I burst with tears of desire to be alone with him.

And, if you ever need a friend, like Joseph Scriven found out, Jesus is the only one that I can wholeheartedly recommend to you. I have no reservations at all. Trust him and he will see you through life's trials and difficulties. What would I do without a friend like this Jesus? I do not know, but I do know that I have found the most valuable and meaningful relationship with him alone. I would be very glad to hear from you about your commitment to the friendship that is found in Jesus Christ. I promise to reply to your personal letter if you write to me today.

My mailing address is:

P. O. 50317
Washington D.C. 20091
U.S.A.

# NOTES

## *Chapter One*: Everyone Needs a Real Friend

1. Dale Carnegie, *How to Win Friends and Influence People* (New York: Pocket Books, 1964), i-iii. As of 1981, this book had sold 15 million copies.

2. Vance Packard, *A Nation of Strangers* (New York: David McKay Co, 1972), 153-154.

3. Ibid, 149.

4. Ibid, 224.

5. Mark Mathabane, *Kaffir Boy: The True Story of a Black Youth's Coming of Age in Apartheid South Africa* (New York: Collier Books, 1989), 20.

6. Ibid.

7. Marlin Carothers, *Prison To Praise* (Escondido, CA: Foundations of Praise, 1992), 1.

8. Charles W. Colson, *Born Again* (Grand Rapids, MI: Spire Books, 1976), 249.

9. Ibid, 254

10. Ibid, 271-272.

11. Mary Rose McGeady, *God's Lost Children: Letters from Covenant House* (New York: Covenant House, 1991), see the dedication.

12. Dee Brestin, *The Friendship of Women* (Wheaton, I1: Victor Books, 1988), 40-41.

13. James Osterhouse, *Bonds of Iron: Forging Lasting Male Relationships* (Chicago, I1 Moody Press, 1994), 7.

14. Ibid, 91-94.

15. Muriel James and Louis M. Savary, *The Heart of Friendship* (New York: Harper & Row, 1978), 86-109.

16. Packard, 6.

## *Chapter Two*: The Meaning of a Real Friend

1. Cited in *The Oxford Dictionary of Quotations,* 3rd ed., (Oxford: University Press, 1980), 553.

2. Cited in Tryon Edwards, compl., *The New Dictionary of Thoughts* (n.p.: Stanbook Inc., 1977), 223.

3. Ibid.

4. Ibid.

5.  Patricia Dreier, *The Gold of Friendship: A Bouquet of Special Thoughts* (Norwalk, CT: The C.R. Gibson Co., 1980) and Hal I. Larson, *You Are My Friend: A Celebration of Friendship* (San Francisco, CA: Halo Books, 1991).

6.  This date is derived from Joan Comay, *Who's Who in the Old Testament* (New York: Oxford University Press, 1993), 319. Other scholars date his rule between 968 and 928 B.C.

7.  The discussion that follows is based upon his essay, *"On Friendship,"* found in *Letters of Marcus Tullius Cicero and Gaius Plinius Caecilius Secundus,* ed., Charles W. Eliot, *The Harvard Classic,* vol. 9 (New York: P.F. Collier and Son, 1956), 9-44.

8.  Ibid, 16.

9.  Ibid, 20

10. Ibid, 15-16.

11. Ibid, 17.

12. Ibid, 27-28.

13. Ibid, 29.

14. Ibid.

15. Ibid, 30.

16. Ibid, 17.

17. Ibid, 35.

18. Ibid, 37.

19. R.B.Y. Scott, *The Anchor Bible: Proverbs, Ecclesiastes – Introduction, Translation, and Notes* (Garden City, NY: Doubleday and Co., 1958), 9-13. See also *The Interpreter's Bible, vol. 4: Psalms, Proverbs* ed., George A. Buttrick (New York: Abingdon Press, 1955), 817-937.

20. I am indebted to Allen P. Ross "Proverbs," in *The Expositor's Bible Commentary*, vol. 5 ed., Frank Gaebelen (Grand Rapids, MI: Zondervan Publishing House, 1991), 883-1134 for Solomon's fourteen points on friendship.

21. The following discussion on Michel Eyquem de Montaigne is based upon his essay published in *Literary and Philosophical Essays*, ed., Charles W. Eliot, *The Harvard Classics*, vol. 32 (New York: P.F. Collier and Son, 1938), 72-86.

22. Ibid, 84.

23. Ibid, 73.

24. Ibid, 75.

25. Ibid, 79.

26. Ibid, 81.

27. Ibid, 81-82.

28. Ibid, 85.

29. C.S. Lewis, *The Four Loves* (San Diego, CA: Harcourt Brace and Co., 1991), 31-56.

30. Ibid, 91-92ff.

31. Ibid, 116-141.

32. The discussion which follows is based upon my understanding of C. S. Lewis, pages 57-90. Quotations are from these pages.

33. Ibid, 126

## *Chapter Three*: Friendship in Lonely America

1. Jacqueline Olds, Richard S. Schwartz and Harriet Webster, *Overcoming Loneliness in Everyday Life* (New York: Carol Publishing Group, 1996), Louise Bernikow, *Alone in America: The Search for Companionship* (New York: Harper & Row, 1986) and Suzanne Gordon, *Lonely in America* (New York: Simon and Schuster, 1976).

2. Tim Hansel, *Through the Wilderness of Loneliness* (Elgin, IL: David C. Cook Publishing Co., 1991), Harold C. Warlick, Jr., *Conquering Loneliness* (Waco, TX: Word Books, 1979), Philip Slater, *The Pursuit of Loneliness: American Culture at the Breaking Point* (Boston: Beacon Press, 1970) and David Riesman, *The Lonely Crowd: A Study of the Changing American*

*Character* (New Haven, CT: Yale University Press, 1966).

3. Cited in Carin Rubenstein and Philip Shaver, *In Search of Intimacy* (New York: Delacorte Press, 1982), 2.

4. Billy Graham, *Newsletter* (August 1986): 3.

5. Bernikow, Hansel, and Elisabeth Elliot have used the terms "desert" and "wilderness" in reference to loneliness. See Elliot, *The Path of Loneliness: It May Seem a Wilderness, But It Can Lead You to God* (Nashville, TN: Thomas Nelson, 1988), 19-23 in Chapter 3.

6. Dan Kiley, *Living Together, Feeling Alone: Healing Your Hidden Loneliness* (New York: Prentice Hall Press, 1989).

7. I had touched upon this matter in Emma S. Etuk, *A Walk Through the Wilderness* (New York: Carlton Press, 1990), 110-126. On the contention that loneliness affects everyone, see all the works cited above including Vance Packard, *A Nation of Strangers,* op. cit., 192-204 and Lillian B. Rubin, *Intimate Strangers: Men and Women Together* (New York: Harper & Row, 1984).

8. Gordon, 25.

9. Ibid, 28.

10. Ibid, 45-193.

11. Ibid, 29.

12. Bernikow, 3.

13. Ibid, 10.

14. Ibid, 11.

15. Ibid.

16. Rubenstein and Shaver, 3.

17. Ibid, 8-14.

18. Kiley, 42.

19. Ibid, 16.

20. Warlick, Jr., 26.

21. Hansel, 21-22 and 29.

22. Clark E. Moustakas, *Loneliness and Love* (Englewood Cliffs, NJ: Prentice Hall, 1972), 130. See also his other book, *The Touch of Loneliness* (Englewood Cliffs, NJ: Prentice Hall, 1975), 21 and 87 and Jeremy Seabrook, *Loneliness* (New York: Universe Books, 1975), 9.

23. Hansel, 29.

24. Dag Hammarskjold, *Markings* (New York: Alfred A. Knopf, 1969), 8 and 85.

25. Ibid., xv and Henry P. Van Dusen, *Dag Hammarskjold: The Statesman and His Faith* (New York: Harper & Row, 1967), 74.

26. Van Dusen, 73 and 75-77.

27. Cited in James and Savary, *The Heart of Friendship*, 99.

28. Van Dusen, 79-84.

29. Hammarskjold, 82.

30. Osterhaus, *Bonds of Iron*, 37-38.

31. Nnamdi Azikiwe, *My Odyssey: An Autobiography* (London: C. Hurst and Co., 1970), 96-104.

32. Emma S. Etuk, *Destiny is not a Matter of Chance: Essays in Reflection and Contemplation on the Destiny of Blacks* (New York: Peter Lang, 1989), 123.

33. Robert Bolton, *People Skills: How to Assert Yourself, Listen to Others, and Resolve Conflicts* (Englewood Cliffs, NJ: Prentice Hall, 1979), 5.

34. Rubenstein and Shaver, 18 and 33-37.

35. Etuk, *A Walk Through the Wilderness*, 111.

36. James L. Lynch, *The Broken Heart: The Medical Consequences of Loneliness* (New York: Basic Books, 1977), 205.

37. Rubenstein and Shaver, 100-106.

38. Earl A. Grollman, *Suicide, Prevention, Intervention, and Postvention* (Boston: Beacon Press, 1971), 117-119 and 140.

39. Kiley, 105.

40. Rubenstein and Shaver, 199-202.

41. Janice G. Raymond, *A Passion for Friends: Toward a Philosophy of Female Affection* (Boston: Beacon Press, 1986).

42. Gordon, 308-309.

43. Rubenstein and Shaver, 202. See also page 172 for a list of positive responses to loneliness.

44. Julie Keene and Ione Jensen, "Going Solo," *The News-Journal* [Daytona Beach, Florida], April 1, 1996, 1C, and their book, *Women Alone: Creating a Joyous and Fulfilling Life* (Carson, CA: Hay House, 1995). See also Rae Andre, *Positive Solitude: A Practical Program for Mastering Loneliness and Achieving Self-Fulfillment* (San Francisco, CA: Harper Collins, 1992), and Lewis M. Andrews, *To Thy Own Self Be True* (New York: Doubleday, 1989).

45. Judith Viorst, *Necessary Losses: The Loves, Illusions, Dependencies, and Impossible Expectations that All of Us Have to Give Up in Order to Grow* (New York: Simon and Schuster, 1986), 182.

## *Chapter Four*: **Woman-to -Woman Friendships**

1. J.F. Allen, *The New Illustrated Children's Bible in Stories* (Nashville, TN: Royal Pubhishers, Inc., 1970), 165.

2. Joel D. Block and Diane Greenberg, *Women & Friendship* (NY: Franklin Watts, 1985), 1.

3. Luise Eichenbaum and Susie Orbach, *Between Women: Love, Envy and Competition in Women's Friendships* (NY: Viking Penguin, Inc., 1988), 1.

4. Block and Greenberg, 1.

5. Ibid., 9.

6. Lois Wyse, *Women Make the Best Friends: A Celebration* (NY: Simon & Schuster, 1995).

7. Block and Greenberg, 15-18 and 21-30.

8. Wyse, 20.

9. Edith Deen, *All of the Women of the Bible* (NY: Harper & Row, 1988), 81.

10. Ibid, 83.

11. Ibid, 84.

12. Ibid, 82.

13. Ibid.

14. Ibid, 85.

15. Ibid., 87

16. Marjory Zoet Bankson, *Seasons of Friendship: Naomi and Ruth as a Pattern* (San Diego,   CA: LuraMedia, 1987), 43.

17. Eichenbaum and Orbach, 11.  See also their other book, *What do Women Want? Exploding the Myth of Dependency* (NY: Coward McCann, 1983).

18. Eichenbaum and Orbach, 75

19. Block and Greenberg, 14 and 15.

## *Chapter Five*: Man-to-Man Friendships

1.  C.S. Lewis, *The Four Loves,* 57 and F.B. Meyer, *The Life of David: The Man After God's Own Heart,* ed. Lance Wubbels (Lynnwood, WA: Emerald Books, 1995), 45. For a fuller biography of King David see Frank Slaughter, *David, Warrior and King: A Biblical Biography* (Cleveland, OH: The World Publishing Co., 1962).

2.  Finis Jennings Dake, *Dake's Annotated Reference Bible* (Lawrenceville, GA.: Dake Bible Sales, Inc., 1983), 329.

3.  These four qualities are extracted from Meyer, *The Life of David*, 46-48.

4.  Slaughter, 13 and 53-61.

5.  James and Savary, *The Heart of Friendship*, 45.

6.  Ibid, 44 and 46.

7.  Allan Loy McGinnis, *The Friendship Factor: How to Get Closer to the People You Care For* (Minneapolis, MN: Augsburg Publishing House, 1979), 27.

8.  Meyer, *The Life of David*, 57-63.

9.  Susan Jeffers, *Opening Our Hearts to Men* (NY: Fawcett Columbine, 1989), 159.

10. Ibid., 155 and 159-160. See also Patrick Fanning and Matthew McKay, *Being a Man: A Guide to the New Masculinity* (Oakland, CA: New Harbinger Publications, 1993), 111-112 for a list of eight obstacles to male friendships.

11. Jeffers, 124.

12. Ibid., 126. See also Fanning and McKay, 117-121 for a list of six ways to enrich an existing friendship.

13. Stuart Miller, *Men and Friendship* (Los Angeles, CA: Jeremy P. Tarcher, Inc., 1983), 179-188; Steven Farmer, *The Wounded Male* (NY: Ballantine Books, 1991), 78-109; Helen M. Reid and Gary Alan Fine, "Self-Disclosure in Men's Friendships: Variations

Associated with Intimate Relations," in Peter M. Nardi, ed. *Men's Friendships* (Newbury Park, CA: Sage Publications, 1992), 132-152. See also James W. Pennebaker, *Opening Up: The Healing Power of Confiding in Others* (NY: William Morrow & Co., 1990).

14. See Caroline J. Simon, "Just Friends, Friends and Lovers, or ...?" *Philosophy and Theology* 82 (Winter 1995): 113-128 and Lillian B. Rubin, *Just Friends: The Role of Friendship in our Lives* (NY: Harper and Row, 1985).

15. Marion F. Solomon, *Lean on Me: The Power of Positive Dependency in Intimate Relationships* (NY: Simon and Schuster, 1994), 23 and 26.

16. Miller, 129.

17. Ibid, 129-142.

18. I recommend that one reads Floyd McClung, *Finding Friendship with God: An Invitation to Intimacy with the Most Important Person in the Universe* (Ann Arbor, MI: Servant Publications, 1992); Tilden Edwards *Spiritual Friend* (NY: Paulist Press, 1980) and James Osterhaus, *Bonds of Iron*, 133-149, "Spirituality: Friendship with God and with People."

19. Edwin Louis Cole, *Maximized Manhood: A Guide To Family Survival* (Dallas, TX: Whitaker House, 1982), 35. See also Fanning and McKay, 115-117 for nine ways to make new make friendships.

## *Chapter Six*: Friendships in the Home

1. Ruth Westheimer and Ben Yagoda, *The Value of Family: A Blueprint for the 21ˢᵗ Century* (NY: Warner Books, 1996), 30-31.

2. Ibid, 31.

3. Ibid, 33.

4. Reuven Bar-Levav, *Every Family Needs a C.E.O: What Mothers and Fathers Can Do About Our Deteriorating Families and Values* (NY: Fathering Inc., 1995), 11.

5. Maggie Gallagher, *The Abolition of Marriage: How We Destroy Lasting Love* (Washington, D. C: Regnery Publishing, 1996), 5.

6. Dan Quayle and Diane Medved, *The American Family: Discovering the Values that Make Us Strong* (NY: HarperCollins, 1996), 2 and 269-277.

7. Thomas Moore, *SoulMates: Honoring the Mysteries of Love and Relationship* (NY: HarperCollins, 1994), 71.

8. Amy E. Dean, *Caring for the Family Soul* (NY: Berkley Books, 1996), 92. For more of this spiritual emphasis on the family, see Hugh and Gayle Prather, *Spiritual Parenting: A Guide to Understanding and Nurturing the Heart of Your Child* (NY: Harmony Books, 1996).

9. Dean, 92-93.

10. Westheimer and Yagoda, 29.

11. Ibid.

12. See David Blankenhorn, *Fatherless America: Confronting Our Most Urgent Social Problem* (NY: Basic Books, 1995): Hillary R. Clinton, *It Takes a Village: And Other Lessons Children Teach Us* (NY: Simon and Schuster, 1995 and William J. Bennett, *The De-Valuing of Family: The Fight for Our Culture and Our Children* (NY: Simon and Schuster, 1994).

13. Block and Greenberg, *Women & Friendship*, 139.

14. Eichenbaum and Orbach, *Between Women*, 185-186.

15. Ibid, 69.

16. Block and Greenberg, 131.

17. Ibid, 132.

18. Ibid, 130.

19. Ibid, 137.

20. Claire Rabin, *Equal Partners – Good Friends: Empowering Couples Through Therapy* (London: Routledge, 1996), 59-83.

21. Block and Greenberg, 132.

22. Ibid, 45.

23. See Susan Forward, *Toxic Parents: Overcoming Their Hurtful Legacy and Reclaiming Your Life* (NY: Bantam Books, 1990).

24. See John Leopold Weil, *Early Deprivation of Empathic Care* (Madison: International Universities Press, 1992) and Heather Smith, *Unhappy Children: Reasons and Remedies* (London: Free Association Books, 1995).

25. Patrick Fanning and Matthew McKay, *Being a Man*, 179-180. See also "The New Narcissism," in Rollo May, *Freedom and Destiny* (NY: Dell Publishing Co., 1981, reprint. 1989), 135-147.

26. Joan Lachkar, *The Narcissistic/Borderline Couple: A Psychoanalytic Perspective on Marital Treatment* (NY: Brunner/Mazel Publishers, 1992), 1 and 3.

27. Stephanie Donaldson-Pressman and Robert M. Pressman, *The Narcissistic Family: Diagnosis and Treatment* (NY: Lexington Books, 1994), 4.

28. Block and Greenberg, 46.

29. Smith, *Unhappy Children*, see backcover flyer.

30. Rollo May cited in Max Cohen and Donald Cohen, *My Father, My Son* (Bethel, CT: Rutledge Books, 1996), backcover flyer.

31. Bar-Levav, 11.

32. Victoria Secunda, *Women and Their Fathers: The*

*Sexual and Romantic Impact of the First Man in Your Life* (NY: Dell Publishing, 1992), 4. See also Robert L. Griswold, *Fatherhood in America: A History* (NY: Basic Books, 1993).

33. Secunda, *When You and Your Mother Can't be Friends: Resolving the Most Complicated Relationship of Your Life* (NY: Dell Publishing, 1990), 315.

34. Rodney S. Patterson, "Male Bonding: Men Relating to Men," in Lee N. June and Matthew Parker, eds. *Men to Men: Perspectives of Sixteen African-American Christian Men* (Grand Rapids, MI: Zondervan Publishing House, 1996), 86. See also Claude L. Dallas, Jr., "The Meaning of Fatherhood," in June and Parker, *Men to Men*, 131-147.

35. See also Patrick J. McDonald and Claudette M. McDonald, *Can Your Marriage be a Friendship?* (NY: Paulist Press, 1996).

36. Mary Pipher, *Reviving Ophelia: Saving the Selves of Adolescent Girls* (NY: Ballantine Books, 1994), 12 and also backcover flyer.

37. William J. Bennett, ed. *The Book of Virtues: A Treasury of Great Moral Stories* (NY: Simon and Schuster, 1993), 269-270.

38. Susan Alexander Yates, *A House Full of Friends: How to Like the Ones You Love* (Colorado Springs, CO: Focus on the Family Publishing, 1995), 6-10 and 95-108.

39. Derek S. Hopson and Darlene Powell Hopson, *Friends, Lovers, and Soul Mates: A Guide to Better Relationships Between Black Men and Women* (NY: Simon and Schuster, 1994), 202.

40. Karen Lindsey, *Friends as Family* (Boston: Beacon Press, 1981), 1 and 189-208.

41. Yates, 140-147.

42. Ibid, 158-160.

## *Chapter Seven*: **Friendships at the Workplace**

1. Block and Greenberg, *Women & Friendship*, 87.

2. Ibid, 78-96 and see Nathaniel Stewart, *Winning Friends at Work* (NY: Ballantin Books, 1985), backcover flyer.  See also Susanna McMahon, *Having Healthy Relationships* (NY: Dell Publishing, 1996), 181-198 and Robert Bolton and Dorothy Grover Bolton, *Social Style/Management Style: Developing Productive Work Relationships* (NY: American Management Association, 1984).

3. Stewart, 12-15.

4. Ibid, 15-17.

5. Ibid, 21-24.  See also Judith Viorst, *Necessary Losses*, 170-184, for a discussion of other kinds of friends, e.g., "convenience friends."

6. Stewart, 25.

7. Ibid, 27-28.

8. Ibid, 29-30.

9. Ibid, 32-36.

10. Ibid, 55-64.

11. Ibid, 46-50.

12. Karen Lindsey, *Friends as Family*, 209-233.

13. Ibid, 210.

14. Ibid, 211.

15. Ibid, 216-217.

16. Ibid, 221.

17. Ibid, 222.

18. Ibid, 229.

19. Ibid, 233.

20. Block and Greenberg, 78-79.

21. Ibid, 84ff.

22 Lindsey, 235.

## *Chapter Eight*: Friendships At Church

1. Osterhaus, *Bonds of Iron*, 49.

2. Cathy Lechner, "Friends are Friends ... Forever?," *Charisma* 23,2 (September 1997): 82, underlining added for emphasis.

3. Stephen R. Covey, *The 7 Habits of Highly Effective People: Restoring the Character Ethic* (New York: Simon and Schuster, 1989), 117.

4. Ibid.

5. Ibid.

6. Ibid, 118.

7. Ibid, 117.

8. Osterhaus, 38-39.

9. Jacqueline Olds, Richard Schwartz and Harriet Webster, *Overcoming Loneliness in Everyday Life*, 181.

10. See "The Megachurch Resource Guide," *Emerge* 8, 6 (April 1997), insert and Hamil R. Harris, "Growing in Glory," *Emerge* (April 1997): 48-53. The forty megachurches listed are all African-American and are defined as congregations whose membership exceed 3,000. Those listed in this insert include congregations with members below 3,000.

11. Personal interview, February 20, 1998.

12. George Barna, *Finding a Church You can call Home: The Complete Guide to Making One of the Most Significant Decisions of Your Life* (Ventura, CA.: Regal Books, 1992), 11, preface.

13. Ibid, 21.

14. Ibid, 40-41.

15. See Billy Bruce, "Fred Price Triggers Debate Over Racism," *Charisma* 23, 9 (April 1998): 16 and the editorial opinion by Stephen Strang, "Let's Join Fred Price's Crusade," *Charisma* (April 1998): 122. The focus of Price's exposition is racism within the American Church and denominations.

16. Warlick, Jr., *Conquering Loneliness*, 34.

17. Ibid.

18. Ibid, 35.

19. Ibid, 66.

20. David B. Barrett, "Annual Statistical Table on Global Mission: 1997," *World Evangelization*, 78 (May 1997): 16-17.

21. Jim Bakker, *I Was Wrong* (Nashville, TN: Thomas Nelson Publishers, 1996), 225.

22. Ibid, 468.

23. Ibid, 456-466.

24. Ibid, 471.

25. Emma S. Etuk, *A Walk Through the Wilderness*, 83-110.

26. Warlick, 62.

27. See Aelred of Rievaulx, *Spiritual Friendship*, trans. Mary Eugenia Laker (Kalamazoo, MI: Cistercian Publications, 1977), John W. Crossin, *Friendship: The Key to Spiritual Growth* (New York: Paulist Press, 1997), Floyd McClung, *Finding Friendship with God* (Ann Arbor, MI: Servant Publications, 1992), Timothy K. Jones, *Mentor & Friend* (Oxford: Lion Publishing Corp., 1991), Joseph A. Payne, *Befriending: A Self-Guided Retreat for Busy People* (New York: Paulist Press, 1992) and Mary E. Hunt, *Fierce Tenderness: A Feminist Theology of Friendship* (New York: Crossroad, 1991).

28. Paula Riple, *Called to be Friends* (Notre Dame, IN: Ave Marie Press, 1980), 11. See also pages 13-28.

29. Ibid, 14.

30. Rubin, *Just Friends*, 7.

31. Michael W. Smith, *It's Time to be Bold* (Nashville, TN: Word Publishing, 1997), 40.

32. Ibid, 74.

33. Ibid 78.

## 34. *Chapter Nine*: Friendships at Schools and Colleges

1. See "The Killing Season," *Newsweek* (June 1, 1998): 33. See also "The Children of Jonesboro," *U.S. News & World Report* (April 6, 1998): 3, 16, 18, 20, and 22; "A Search for Answers in a Wounded Town," *Newsweek* (April 13, 1998): 36-37; "The Boys Behind the Ambush," *Newsweek* (April 6, 1998): 20-24, and 26. Consider also the articles on pages 25-27

2. See "A Son Who Spun Out of Control," *Newsweek* (June 1, 1998): 32-33 and "Again," *U.S News & World Report* (June 1, 1998): 5, 16-18 and 21.

3. Kit Lively, "Drug Arrests Rise Again," *The Chronicle of Higher Education* 42, 33 (April 26, 1996): A37-A49

4. Melanie Thernstrom, "Diary of a Murder," *The New Yorker* 52,4 (June 3, 1996): 62-71.

5. Colin Powell, "I Wasn't Left to Myself," *Newsweek* (April 27, 1998): 28.

6. Thernstrom, 64.

7. Ibid.

8. Ibid, 70.

9. Ibid, 68.

10. Ibid, 65.

11. Ibid, 66-67.

12. Ibid, 65.

13. Ibid, 66.

14. Ibid, 68.

15. See "More Drug Arrests Reported on Larger College Campuses," *News-Journal* (April 21, 1996): 3A.

16. D'Lena M. Ambrose, "Bowdoin College Shuts 2 Fraternities After Death of Student at Party," *The Chronicle of Higher Education* (April 26, 1996): A49.

17. Michael B. Katz, *Resconstructing American Education* (Cambridge, MA: Harvard University Press, 1987), 166. See also E.D. Hirsch, Jr., *The Schools We Need and Why We Don't Have Them* (NY: Doubleday, 1996), 69-126; Thomas Sowell, *Black Education: Myths and Tragedies* (NY: David McKay Co., 1972) and Herbert H. Hyman, Charles R. Wright and John Shelton, *The Enduring Effects of Education* (Chicago, IL: The University of Chicago Press, 1975).

18. Katz, 42 and 46. Americans were shocked when Jonathan Kozol, *Illiterate America* (Garden City, NY: Anchor Press, 1985) appeared. With television and computers, is it any wonder that our high school graduates cannot spell, memorize, nor can they do their maths without a calculator? Some have defended this trend by pointing out that many American millionaires do not need nor do they have any formal education, e.g., that Bill Gates has no doctorate, so

what?

19. David E. Purpel, *The Moral & Spiritual Crisis in Education: A Curriculum for Justice & Compassion in Education* (Granby, MA: Bergin & Garvey Publishers, 1989), 28. See also pp. 65-69.

20. Julie Grace, "When the Silence Fell," *Time* 150, 25 (December 15, 1997): 54.

21. Ibid.

22. William J. Kreidler, "How Can I Make Friends?" *Instructor* 106, 6 (March 1997): 74-75. See also Doris Bergen, "Facilitating Friendship Development In Inclusion Classrooms," *Childhood Education* 69,4 (Summer 1993): 234-235; Janis R. Bullock, "Children Without Friends: Who Are They and How Can Teachers Help?" *Childhood Education* 69,2 (Winter 1992): 92-97; and Michael R. Conolly, "How Do You Spell Friendship? An International Spelling Bee," *The Clearing House* 66, 5 (May-June 1993): 267-268.

23. Terry Martinez, "Building a Bridge with Special Students," *Instructor* 105, 1 (July-August 1995): 44-46.

24. Ron Rigli, "The A.R.T. Exchange: Americans and Russians Together," *School Arts* 92, 8 (April 1993): 28-29. This is a program in art and friendship between American and Russian students.

## *Chapter Ten*: Friendships Across Racial Lines

1. W.E.B. Dubois, *The Souls of Black Folk* (New York: Bantam, 1989), xxxi.

2. Vivian R. Rouson, "Racism and Religion: President Clinton Joins Crusade for Racial Unity," *The Christian Times International* 1,2 (July 1997): 18. The United States official program on racism initiated by Bill Clinton is called "*Community 2020.*"

3. See Thomas F. Gossett, *Race: The History of an Idea in America* (New York: Schocken Books, 1965), Winthrop D. Jordan, *White Over Black: American Attitudes Toward the Negro*, 1550-1812 (Baltimore, MD: Penguin Books, 1968), Joseph R. Washington, Jr., *Anti-Blackness in English Religion 1500-1800* (New York: The Edwin Mellen Press, 1984) and George M. Frederickson, *The Black Image in the White Mind: The Debate on Afro-American Character and Destiny*, 1817-1914 (New York: Harper & Row, Publishers, 1971).

4. See Derrick A. Bell, *Faces at the Bottom of the Well: The Permanence of Racism in Black America* (New York: Basic Books, 1992), Andrew Hacker, *Two Nations: Black and White, Separate,Hostile,Unequal* (New York: Ballantine Books, 1995), Janet E. Helms, *A Race is a Nice Thing to Have: A Guide to Being a White Person or Understanding the White Persons in Your Life* (Topeka, KS: Content Communications, 1994) and Ivan Hannaford, *Race: The History of an Idea in the West* (Washington, DC: The Woodrow Wilson Center Press, 1996).

5. Gossett, 32.

6. Ronald Sanders, *Lost Tribes and Promised Lands: The Origins of American Racism* (New York: Harper Collins Publishers, 1992), 17.

7. See William Julius Wilson, *The Declining Significance of Race: Blacks and Changing American Institutions* (Chicago, IL: The University of Chicago Press, 1978), 7. See also Ashley Montagu, *Man's Most Dangerous Myth: The Fallacy of Race.* 5th ed. rev & enl. (New York: Oxford University Press, 1974) and *The Concept of Race* (New York: Macmillan, 1964).

8. David Theo Goldberg, *Racial Subjects: Writing on Race in America* (New York: Routledge, 1997), 176. See also Dinesh D'Souza *The End of Racism: Principles for a Multiracial Society* (New York: The Free Press, 1995).

9. Ali Rattansi and Sallie Westwood, eds., *Racism, Modernity and Identity on the Western Front* (Cambridge, MA: Polity Press, 1994), 1.

10. Calvin C. Hernton, *Sex and Racism in America* (New York: Doubleday, 1988), 173.

11. Ibid, 174.

12. Carl T. Rowan, *The Coming Race War in America: A Wake-up Call* (Boston: Little, Brown & Co., 1996).

13. Thomas Sowell, *Race and Culture: A World View* (New York: Basic Books, 1994), 154.

14. Frederickson, cited in D'Souza, 27.

15. D'Souza, 27. See also 561-562.

16. Joseph Barndt, *Dismantling Racism: The Continuing Challenge to White America* (Minneapolis, MN: Augsburg Fortress, 1991), 28.

17. Clyde W. Ford, *We Can All Get Along: 50 Steps You Can Take To Help End Racism* (New York: Dell Publishing, 1994), 11.

18. Hernton, 178.

19. Terry Stull, *The Disease of Racism: Rediscovering the Cure* (Shippensburg, PA: Companion Press, 1996), 3.

20. Paul Kivel, *Uprooting Racism: How White People Can Work for Racial Justice* (Gabriola Island, B.C: New Society Publishers, 1996), 17. See also Kenan Malik, *The Meaning of Race: Race, History and Culture in Western Society* (New York: New York University Press, 1996).

21. Ruth Frankenberg, *White Women, Race Matters: The Social Construction of Whiteness* (Minneapolis: University of Minnesota Press, 1993), 1 and 236. See also Joel Kovel, *White Racism: A Psychohistory* (New York: Columbia University Press, 1984) and Judith H. Katz, *White Awareness: Handbook for Anti-Racism Training* (Norman: University of Oklahoma Press, 1978).

22. Frankenberg, 1.

23. Michael Wieviorka cited in Rattansi and Westwood, 183-185.

24. Hacker, 23 & 24.

25. D'Souza, 121.

26. Barndt, 75-100; Compare with D'Souza, 289-336.

27. Ford, 13-15.

28. Ibid, 33.

29. Stull, 22-23.

30. Barndt, 52.

31. Ibid, 73.

32. Moyibi, Amoda, *Black Politics and Black Vision* (Philadelphia, PA: Westminster Press, 1972, 151-153.

33. Ibid, 151.

34. Hacker, 33.

35. See Jim Sleeper, *Liberal Racism* (New York: Viking, 1997) and Robert Miles, *Racism After 'Race Relations'* (London: Routledge, 1993).

36. Mark and Gail Mathabane, *Love in Black and White;The Triumph of Love Over Prejudice and Taboo* (New York: Harper Colins Publishers, 1992). These quotes are from the back cover.

## *Chapter Eleven*: **The Benefits of Friendship**

1. Cited in William J. Bennett, ed., *The Book of Virtues*, 331.

2. See Edwards, *The New Dictionary of Thoughts*, 223.

3. Ibid.

4. Ibid.

5. Ibid, 222.

6. Ibid, 222-223.

7. Hal Larson, *You are my Friend*, 101.

8. Ibid, 117.

9. Cited in Larson, 125 and 131.

10. Cited in Bennett, 329.

11. Cited in Larson, 114.

12. Cited in Edwards, 224.

13. Cited in Larson, 103.

14. Ibid, 113.

15. Cited in Bennett, *Book of Virtues*, 339.

16. Cited in Larson, 114.

17. Cited in Bennett, *Book of Virtues*, 335.

18. Ibid, 336.

19. *Guideposts*, Calendar, 1998.

20. Cited in Larson, 115.

21. Bennett, *Book of Virtues*, 269.

22. Cited in Edwards, 222.

23. Ibid, 225.

24. Ibid, 222.

25. Cited in Bennett, *Book of Virtues*, 342. See also Cathy Lechner, "Friends are Friends ... Forever?," *Charisma* 23, 2 (September 1997): 87. She agrees that "a friend is a great support."

26. Judith Viorst, *Necessary Losses*, 182.

27. Ibid, 178. See also Osterhaus, *Bonds of Iron*, 61.

28. Bennett, *Book of Virtues*, 306-308.

29. Ibid, 284.

30. Ibid, 269.

31. Carin Rubenstein and Phillip Shaver, *In Search of Intimacy*, 33-37.

32. Ibid. For their analysis of "Childhood Roots of

Loneliness," see pp. 38-61.

33.  Etuk, *A Walk Through the Wilderness*, 126-128.

34.  James Patterson and Peter Kim, *The Day America Told the Truth*, 72.

35.  Lillian B. Rubin, *Just Friends*, 111-112.

36.  Ibid, 113-114.

37.  Walter Trobisch, *I Loved a Girl* (New York: HarperCollins, 1989).  It first appeared in 1963.  It is now a classic.

38.  Bari-Ellen Roberts, *Roberts vs Texaco: A True Story of Race and Corporate America* (New York: Avon Books, 1998), x.

39.  See Lechner, 82, underlining added for emphasis.

40.  Paula Ripple, *Called to be Friends*, 53.

41.  Ibid, 41.

42.  Ibid, 52.

43.  Rubin, 34-54.

44.  James and Savary, 41-43.

45.  Carmen L. Caltagirone, *Friendship as a Sacrament* (State Island, NY:  Alba House, 1988), 83.

46.  Barbara Powell, *Good Relationships are Good Medicine*

(Emmaus, PA: Rodale Press, 1987), 6, underlining added for emphasis.

47.  Dan P. McAdams, *Intimacy: The Need to be Close* (New York: Doubleday, 1989), 127 and 130.

48.  Allan Loy McGinnis, *The Friendship Factor*, 15.

49.  Lynch, 181.

50.  Ibid, 65.

51.  Ibid, 68.

52.  McGinnis, 15.

## *Chapter Twelve*: Conclusion

1.  Isidore cited in Jim Haak Adels, *The Wisdom of the Saints: An Anthology* (New York: Oxford University Press, 1987), 138.

2.  Floyd McClung, *Finding Friendship with God*, 33-34.

# ABOUT THE AUTHOR

Author, speaker, and a professional historian, Emma S. Etuk is the founder and director of Nigeria for Christ Ministries. A graduate of Howard University in Washington, D.C., he obtained a Ph.D. in United States History, with minors in African History and International Relations.

Formerly a civil servant, Etuk attended the Polytechnic, Calabar, in Nigeria, where he received a Higher National Diploma in Estate Management. He also received a B.A. degree in Business Administration from Malone College, Canton, Ohio; M.A. in Church History from Ashland Theological Seminary; and did graduate work at the Institute of Church and State at Baylor University in Waco, Texas.

A motivational speaker, Etuk has taught history at Howard, Dillard, and Morgan State universities, as well as at Bethune-Cookman College. He has lectured in Nigeria and in the United States, and has written four books, several articles and essays which have been widely read.

He is currently a patron-member and Vice-President for Africa of the International Society of Friendships and Good Will (ISFGW). He is also a member of the Friendship Force, Inc., a husband, and father of two lovely children. He conducts seminars and lectures on Christian evangelism, soul-winning techniques and on the topics related to his books. *Friends* is his fifth book.

# INDEX

Advice, 79
Affection, 72
Ally, 207
Approval, 80
Aristotle, 202
Assistance, 208
Assurance, 82
Availability, 81
Azikiwe, Nnamdi, 48

Bacon, Francis, 202
Bakker, Jim, 138

Carnegie, Dale, 1-2
Childhood development, 209
Christ, Jesus, 226-227
Church leader, 147-152

Church shopping, 134, 135
Cicero, M. Tullius, 19-26, 111, 201, 202
Clinton, Hillary, 96, 161
College, 172-176
Colson, Chuck, 10
Communication, 100
Confidence, 2
Covenant, 77

David, 69, 74-75
Democracy. 149
Divorce, 51
Dobson, James, 105
DuBois, W. E. B., 69, 178

Education, 167-172
Emerson, R. Waldo, 203
Euripides, 18, 202

Fairness, 101
Faith, 73
Family, 96
  extended type, 108-110
  single-parent, 94
Fathers, 105, *see also*
  parents
Female friendship, 55-57,
64
Fondness, 78
Franklin, Benjamin, 217
Friendlessness,
  effect of, 9
  of prison life, 12
Friends, 3
  society of, 35, 153
Friendship, 101
  blessings of, 25
  characteristics of, 21,
33, 142
  child-parent type, 102
  among children, 106-
108
  at church, 129, 133
  definition of, 21, 33
  enhancing, 126
  extended family, 108-
110
  female type, 55-57, 64

husband-wife type, 97-
102
  impediments of, 78
  kinds of, 31, 120
  inter-racial type, 196
  male type, 69
  to newcomers, 3
  permanence of, 28, 30
  qualities of, 73, 121,
224
  reasons for, 143
  rules of, 25
  sign of, 29
  spiritual, 140-143
  test of, 24
  universal need of, 2
  at workplace, 111

Graham, Billy, 41

Home, 110, 95
Humility, 86

Infatuation, 100

Jefferson, Thomas, 192,
205
Jonathan, 70, 71

Kissing, 29, 87

Lewis, C. Staples, 19, 32-
37, 70, 155
Liberation, 217, 218

Loneliness, 39, 42, 44-46, 49, 220
  anguish of, 40
  antidone for, 52, 205
  cost of, 50
  as a disease, 44
  meaning of, 43
  problem of, 40, 51
Longevity, 218
Love, 63, 64, 150, 198, 213
  catalyst for, 211
  intensity of , 214
  notions of, 211-212
Loyalty, 24
Luther, Martin, 191, 195

Madison, James, 205
Male friendship, 69
Maslow, Abraham, 215
Maturity, 72
Montainge, Michel de, 19, 30-32
Murphy, Eddie, 7

Naomi, 58, 61, 62
Napoleon, 204
Networking, 221

Parent, 167
  toxic type, 102-103
Pastors, 151
Plato, 18, 202
Powell, Colin, 160

Prayer, 84, 151, 226
Protection, 78

Race, 179-184
  meaning of, 179
Racism, 48, 178-198
  consequences of, 194
  definition of, 183, 184
  as a disease, 185
  Father of, 181
  kinds of, 185, 187-193
  levels of, 186-187
  problem of, 64
  as a sin, 195, 197
Racist, 178, 184-191, 195
Relationship,
  categories of, 32
  platonic type, 3
Restoration, 81
Ruth, 58-60

Quayle, Dan, 94

School,
  related killings, 155-158
  religious instructions in, 169
Self-disclosure, 83
Self-esteem, 2, 24
Security, 78
Sensitivity, 72

Sexual harrassment, 117
Shakespeare, William, 203
Society of friends, 35, 153
Socrates, 203
Solomon, 19, 26-30
Spontaneity, 76
Surrender, 76

Tenderness, 72
Toxic parents, 102-103
Transparency, 83, 84

University, 177 *see also* college
Vision of meaning, 169

Women's Therapy Center, 56